I0453958

SELF-CARE AND EMOTIONAL EMPOWERMENT FOR BLACK WOMEN

THE ULTIMATE MENTAL HEALTH GUIDE TO CONQUER NEGATIVE SELF-TALK AND INTERNALIZED OPPRESSION TO HEAL, GROW, AND THRIVE

JADA AMARI

ISBN: 978-1-953149-50-3
Published by: Jada Amari
© Copyright 2023 - All rights reserved.

All rights reserved. No part of this publication may be reproduced, distributed, or transmitted in any form or by any means, including photocopying, recording, or other electronic or mechanical methods, without the prior written permission of the publisher, except in the case of brief quotations embodied in critical reviews and certain other noncommercial uses permitted by copyright law.

Under no circumstances will any blame or legal responsibility be held against the publisher, or author, for any damages, reparation, or monetary loss due to the information contained within this book, either directly or indirectly.

Legal Notice:

This book is copyright protected. It is only for personal use. You cannot amend, distribute, sell, use, quote or paraphrase any part, or the content within this book, without the consent of the author or publisher.

Disclaimer Notice:

Please note the information contained within this document is for educational and entertainment purposes only. All effort has been executed to present accurate, up to date, reliable, and complete information. No warranties of any kind are declared or implied.

Readers acknowledge that the author is not engaged in the rendering of legal, financial, medical, or professional advice. The content within this book has been derived from various sources. Please consult a licensed professional before attempting any techniques outlined in this book.

By reading this document, the reader agrees that under no circumstances is the author responsible for any losses, direct or indirect, that are incurred as a result of the use of the information contained within this document, including, but not limited to, errors, omissions, or inaccuracies.

CONTENTS

Are you tired of the endless diet culture and ready to cultivate a more positive and mindful relationship with food?

This comprehensive guide offers tips, strategies, and exercises for practicing mindful eating to promote physical and emotional health.

From healthy recipes to nutritional advice, you'll find everything you need to nourish your body and mind with intention and care.

Say goodbye to mindless snacking and hello to a more balanced and positive relationship with food.

- Unleash the Hidden Potential Within You and Unlock the Key to Abundance!
- Discover the Secrets to Manifesting the Life You Deserve Through the Power of the Universe.
- Experience a Life of Limitless Opportunities and Overcome Your Deepest Fears and Doubts.
- Open the Door to Unlimited Happiness, Success, and Abundance with These Powerful Tips and Techniques!

Join a movement of Black women who are determined to achieve greatness and help others do the same. From daily habits and self-care routines to career advice and financial literacy, we've got you covered.

Scan Me

INTRODUCTION

"Each time a woman stands up for herself, she stands up for all women." - Maya Angelou

Have you ever felt like you just can't shake the negative thoughts in your head? The ones that tell you you're not good enough, smart enough, or strong enough? Or maybe you've internalized all the messages you've heard growing up in a world that often doesn't see the value in black women like us

Well, let me tell you, you're not alone. Studies have shown that a significant number of black women struggle with negative self-talk and internalized oppression. So many of us have faced these same struggles and come out on the other side stronger and more resilient.

As a black woman who has been on a similar journey, I know that life can be tough, but I also know that we are meant for greatness. That's why I wrote this book, just for us.

Now, I'm not going to tell you that this journey of self-love and emotional empowerment is going to be easy. It's going to be hard, and it's going to take work. But let me tell you, it's worth it.

In fact, I want you to meet Jasmine...

Jasmine is a black woman who has always struggled with negative self-talk. She couldn't seem to escape the little voice in her head that constantly told her she wasn't good enough. She would hear things like "you're not smart enough" or "you're not pretty enough" and it was exhausting.

Jasmine grew up in a world that told her that as a black woman, she had to work twice as hard to get half as far. And she believed it. For years, she would push herself to her limits, trying to prove herself to the world. But no matter how hard she tried, it never seemed to be enough.

Jasmine knew that she had to make a change. She started by reading books and watching videos about self-love and self-care. She found that she was not alone in this journey and began to make positive changes in her life.

She started to challenge her negative self-talk and replace it with positive affirmations. Jasmine began to practice mindfulness and self-care, making time to do the things that made her happy. She started setting boundaries, realizing that it was okay to say no to things that didn't serve her.

As she continued on this journey of self-discovery and self-love, Jasmine found that she was healing from the trauma and wounds of her past. She began to build healthy relationships, embrace her body, and celebrate her blackness.

Now, Jasmine is a woman who knows her worth. She still faces challenges, but she has the tools and techniques to overcome them. She's happier and more confident than ever before.

Jasmine's story isn't the only one. Throughout this book, I will continue to share stories of black women who were in the same boat as you, feeling stuck, oppressed, and defeated. But guess what? They turned it around and found the power within themselves to heal and grow. And you can too!

You'll begin to see what's possible when you work on yourself, your mental health, and build a supportive community with other black women on a similar path.

This self-love workbook is all about helping you take control of your mental, physical, and emotional well-being. We'll explore various topics, such as mindfulness, setting boundaries, healing from trauma, building confidence, body positivity, relationship navigation, and even financial empowerment. With exercises, journal prompts, and reflective moments, I'm going to be your personal cheerleader on this journey of self-discovery and self-love.

As the great Audre Lorde once said, "Caring for myself is not self-indulgence, it is self-preservation, and that is an act of political warfare." Embracing this philosophy, we'll see the intersection of self-love and blackness and learn how to overcome any internalized oppression.

My goal is to create a safe and empowering space for us to explore, heal, and grow. I want you to know that you deserve love, happiness, and success, and together, we can break down the barriers that have held us back for far too long.

And remember, self-love isn't a finish line, it's a journey, and one worth taking, hand in hand!

Are you ready to join the sisterhood of self-care and emotional empowerment for black women?

If so, turn the page, and let's begin this transformative journey together.

CHAPTER 1
SELF-LOVE AND ITS IMPORTANCE FOR BLACK WOMEN

"Love yourself first and everything else falls into line." - Lucille Ball

You're amazing, girl, and you deserve all the love in the world! But sometimes, it can be hard to show yourself that love. That's why we're going to talk about the importance of self-love and why it's especially vital for black women.

This is one of my favorite topics because it's so critical to our overall well-being. You see, as black women, we have a lot of historical baggage that we carry around with us, from slavery and segregation to modern-day microaggressions. And it can all weigh on us heavily. That's why we need to make sure we prioritize self-love.

It's about treating yourself with kindness, compassion, and respect. Self-love is essential for our overall well-being and mental health. It's especially important for black women to prioritize self-love, as we often face societal pressures, discrimination, and oppression.

Self-love is not only about feeling good about ourselves, but it's also about being able to take care of ourselves. When we love ourselves, we are able to set healthy boundaries, make decisions that align with our values, and have a sense of self-worth.

In this chapter, we'll explore the connection between self-love and mental health and discuss the different aspects of self-love. We'll also examine how self-love affects our ability to take care of ourselves.

I'm excited to show you a whole new perspective on what it means to love yourself as a black woman.

So, grab a pen and let's get started!

SARAH'S STORY

Have you ever felt like you weren't enough despite all your achievements? You're not alone. Sarah, a high-achieving black woman, knows exactly how that feels.

Sarah was always a top-performing student who participated in multiple extracurricular activities. She was determined to succeed and had a bright future ahead of her. However, even with all her accomplishments, she couldn't shake off the nagging voice in her head that told her she wasn't good enough. She felt like she had to work harder than everyone else to prove her worth.

It wasn't until Sarah started therapy that she realized she was a victim of internalized oppression. She had internalized all the negative messages and stereotypes that society propagates about black women, and they were affecting her mental health. But through therapy, Sarah learned to recognize these negative thoughts and to focus on her own worth and value.

Sarah began to practice self-care and positive affirmations, reminding herself of all the amazing things she had accomplished and all the unique qualities that made her special. She realized that her worth was not based on external achievements but on her intrinsic value as a human being.

Over time, Sarah's negative thoughts diminished, and she was able to see herself in a new light. Today, Sarah is a successful businesswoman who uses her platform to speak out about the importance of mental health and self-care for black women. She is a living testament to the power of therapy, self-care, and self-love.

Sarah's story is a powerful reminder that we are not defined by our external achievements or by society's expectations of us. Our worth and value come from within, and it's up to us to recognize and nurture that worth.

SELF-LOVE AND ITS IMPORTANCE FOR BLACK WOMEN

Self-love is a way of thinking that allows us to appreciate and be proud of ourselves, despite any imperfections or personal experiences that have shaped us. It's about accepting ourselves and our worth and not allowing others to make us feel bad about who we are.

As black women, we have been programmed to idolize White European beauty, which often leads to negative thoughts and self-hate. This has become so ingrained in our subconscious that we have come to believe it as truth. Unfortunately, this self-hating process has led to alarming rates of suicide among black women.

Did you know that self-love is also critical for our mental health? When we take care of our mental well-being, we can overcome negative thoughts, anxiety, and depression, leading to improved mental health. Practicing self-love helps us embrace our strengths and weaknesses, which allows us to move forward with confidence and resilience.

It's crucial for us to love ourselves, especially since others refuse to see our worth. Self-love is a powerful way of thinking that allows us to take control of our minds. We must learn to believe in our potential to tame "negative self-talk" and internalized oppression. By eliminating our negative thoughts, we can stop feeling inadequate and scared of who we are becoming.

When you catch yourself thinking negatively about your appearance or your abilities, try replacing those thoughts with positive affirmations such as "I am beautiful just the way I am" or "I am capable and deserving of success." It's important to remember that self-love is not just about feeling good about yourself, but it's also about taking care of your mental health.

Let's learn to appreciate and love ourselves for who we are, flaws and all. Let's embrace our strengths and weaknesses, and let's not allow others to make us feel bad about ourselves. Let's take control of our minds and overcome negative thoughts and internalized oppression. Together, we can create a community of strong, confident, and empowered black women who love themselves and each other.

BENEFITS OF CULTIVATING SELF-LOVE

As black women, it's essential that we prioritize our own well-being and happiness to thrive and succeed in our personal and professional lives. One of the best ways to do that is by loving ourselves fully and unconditionally.

When you love yourself, it can positively impact various aspects of your life, including your relationships with your children, friends, and community. It can help you heal from emotional pain, understand your worth, and build your confidence.

Let's explore some other benefits of cultivating self-love:

Becoming a better parent

First and foremost, self-love can help us become better parents, honey. When we love and respect ourselves, we can model that behavior for our children and teach them how to love and respect themselves too. For example, when you're feeling overwhelmed and need some alone time, it's important to communicate that to your children in a healthy and compassionate way. This shows them that it's okay to take care of ourselves and sets a good example for them to follow.

Now, I know it's not always easy, sis. As black women, we often neglect our own needs and put our children's needs first. We've been taught that being a good mother means sacrificing our own happiness for the sake of our children. But the truth is, our children need us to be happy and fulfilled so that we can be there for them in the best way possible.

When we neglect our own needs, we're not showing our children the love and attention they deserve. Our families need to be happy and full of love, and the best way to achieve this is by practicing self-love. By taking care of ourselves, we can be present for our children and give them the attention they need to thrive.

Healing from emotional pain

Self-love also allows us to heal from emotional pain. When we learn to love ourselves, we can let go of past hurts and move forward with a positive outlook on life. For example, if you've experienced a traumatic event in the past, self-love can help you process those emotions and release them, so you no longer give them power over your present and future.

Understanding your value

Understanding your value is another significant benefit of self-love. When we love ourselves, we can dispel the myth that we're not good enough or that something is wrong with us because we're black women. We can recognize our unique abilities and talents and appreciate ourselves for who we are, without comparing ourselves to others.

Developing empathy and compassion

Developing empathy and compassion is also a benefit of self-love. When we love ourselves, we can understand the struggles of others and connect with them on a deeper level. We can build meaningful relationships with our friends and community by showing them the same kindness and compassion that we show ourselves.

Encouraging physical activity

Self-love can also encourage us to engage in physical activity and take care of our bodies. For example, instead of seeing exercise as a chore, we can appreciate the joy of moving our bodies and feeling strong and healthy.

Setting higher standards for dating

Setting higher standards for dating is another benefit of self-love. When we love and respect ourselves, we won't settle for less in our relationships with men. We can recognize a good man when we see one and turn away from those who don't meet our standards.

Boosting career confidence

Self-love can also boost our confidence in our careers. When we love ourselves, we believe in our abilities and know that we have what it takes to succeed in any situation. We can approach job interviews and career opportunities with confidence and self-assurance.

Recognizing the importance of community

When we love and respect ourselves, we can recognize the value of helping and giving back to our community, which can be incredibly rewarding. We understand that by doing our part and making a positive impact on the world around us, we not only benefit ourselves, but we can also help others in need.

In addition to this, self-love can bring black women together, fostering a community of respect and love for each other. Instead of tearing each other down, we can build each other up, recognizing that we all have value and worth. By supporting and empowering each other, we can create a network of strong, confident, and compassionate women who are united in their love for themselves and each other.

Avoiding abusive relationships

Self-love also helps us avoid abusive relationships. When we love and respect ourselves, we won't tolerate abuse or mistreatment from others. We can set boundaries and communicate our needs and expectations in our relationships with men.

Attracting positive relationships

Attracting positive relationships is another benefit of self-love. When we love ourselves, we radiate positivity and confidence, attracting others who value and appreciate us for who we are.

Overcoming negativity

Overcoming negativity is also a benefit of self-love. When we love ourselves, we can recognize and overcome the negative messages and societal pressures that surround us. We can appreciate our own unique beauty and worth without comparing ourselves to others.

Freeing from internalized oppression

Finally, self-love can free us from internalized oppression. When we love and respect ourselves, we can eradicate racism and other forms of oppression from our hearts and minds, freeing ourselves from the negative messages that have held us hostage.

THE DIFFERENT ASPECTS OF SELF-LOVE

Remember, it is not just about the way we look or our external beauty. It is about accepting ourselves holistically, including our personality, background, and experiences. When we practice self-love, we care for ourselves mentally, emotionally, and physically. Let's explore the different aspects of self-love.

Mental Self-Love

Mental self-love involves taking care of our mental health. We do this by cultivating positive thoughts about ourselves, identifying and challenging negative self-talk, and seeking help when we need it. It is crucial to take care of our mental well-being to stay resilient and focused on our goals.

Emotional Self-Love

Emotional self-love involves accepting and acknowledging our emotions without judgment. It means allowing ourselves to feel our emotions fully and expressing them appropriately. Emotional self-love also involves setting boundaries and learning to say no when necessary.

Learning to identify and express emotions is a vital part of emotional self-love. For example, when we feel sad, we should allow ourselves to experience the sadness and take time to process it. We shouldn't try to push it away or suppress it. Instead, we should allow ourselves to cry, talk to a trusted friend or therapist, or engage in self-care activities that help us feel better. By doing this, we validate our emotions, which helps us develop a sense of self-worth and self-respect.

Physical Self-Love

Taking care of our physical health is another significant aspect of self-love. Self-care involves nurturing our physical, emotional, and mental well-being. This can include engaging in activities such as exercise, getting enough sleep, eating well, spending time in nature, meditating, and participating in hobbies and activities that bring us joy. Prioritizing self-care shows that we value ourselves and our health, which, in turn, increases our self-esteem and self-love. So, make sure to take a break and indulge in some self-care activities that make you feel good, both inside and out.

Spiritual Self-Love

Spiritual self-love involves connecting with something greater than ourselves, and finding meaning and purpose in life. It can involve religious or spiritual practices, but it doesn't have to. Spiritual self-love is about developing a sense of inner peace and connecting with our values and beliefs.

Practicing spiritual self-love can involve meditation, mindfulness, or engaging in activities that bring us a sense of purpose and fulfillment. It can also involve connecting with nature, practicing gratitude, or engaging in acts of kindness and compassion towards others.

Social Self-Love

Developing healthy relationships with others is an important aspect of self-love. We should aim to surround ourselves with people who uplift and support us, rather than bringing us down. This can involve spending time with friends and family, joining clubs or organizations that share our interests, or seeking out therapy or support groups to help us navigate difficult relationships.

However, it's important to remember that developing healthy relationships isn't just about others; it's also about how we communicate with them. Effective communication is key to building and maintaining healthy relationships. By communicating our needs and feelings clearly and respectfully, we can develop relationships based on mutual trust and respect. This means being honest with ourselves and others, setting boundaries when necessary, and expressing ourselves respectfully and authentically.

SELF-LOVE IN ACTION

When we encounter challenges or make mistakes, it's important to treat ourselves with kindness and understanding. We must learn to extend the same care and compassion to ourselves that we would offer to a close friend. So, the next time you find yourself being hard on yourself, take a deep breath, and remind yourself that you're only human, and it's okay to make mistakes.

Identifying and expressing our emotions

Many of us have been taught to suppress our emotions, either because we were told that emotions are a sign of weakness, or because we feel uncomfortable with the intensity of our feelings. However, suppressing emotions can be harmful to our mental and physical health. It's essential to allow ourselves to feel our emotions fully and express them appropriately. For example, if you're feeling anxious or stressed, take a moment to acknowledge and validate your emotions. You can try journaling, talking to a friend, or even seeking professional help to process your emotions in a healthy way.

Setting boundaries

Boundaries are necessary to protect our emotional well-being and prevent others from taking advantage of us. Learning to say no is a powerful act of self-love because it shows that we value ourselves and our time. It's important to remember that saying no doesn't make us selfish or mean. It merely means that we're taking care of ourselves, which is a vital part of emotional self-love.

Purpose and meaning in life

When we have something to strive for that aligns with our values and passions, we feel a sense of fulfillment and satisfaction. This can lead to greater self-esteem and self-worth, as we recognize our own strengths and capabilities in pursuing our goals. So, take some time to explore your passions and interests and set goals that align with your values.

Gratitude

By focusing on the things we are thankful for in our lives, we can shift our attention away from negative self-talk and self-criticism. When we appreciate ourselves and what we have, we are more likely to feel content and happy with who we are. Take a moment each day to reflect on the things you're grateful for, whether it's your health, your family, or even something as simple as a warm cup of coffee.

Negative self-talk

By challenging negative self-talk and replacing it with positive affirmations and self-talk, we can shift our mindset and cultivate a more loving and compassionate relationship with ourselves. So, the next time you catch yourself thinking negative thoughts about yourself, replace them with positive affirmations such as "I am worthy" or "I am enough." Remember, the way we talk to ourselves matters, and by changing our self-talk, we can change our perception of ourselves.

Self-forgiveness

We all make mistakes, but holding onto guilt and shame can damage our self-esteem and self-worth. By forgiving ourselves for past mistakes and accepting ourselves as imperfect but worthy, we can cultivate a more loving and compassionate relationship with ourselves. Remember, self-forgiveness is not about excusing our behavior but rather about letting go of the negative emotions that hold us back from loving ourselves fully.

Physical Health

Physical health is a vital aspect of self-love. We've got to treat our bodies with kindness and respect, instead of constantly criticizing and judging them. Prioritizing activities that promote health and well-being is essential for nurturing physical self-love. This includes regular exercise, eating healthily, getting enough sleep, and engaging in activities that bring us joy. When we make our physical self-love a priority, we send a message to ourselves that our health and happiness matter.

Learning to appreciate our bodies is a crucial part of physical self-love. Society often tries to tell us we're not good enough, which can lead to negative self-talk and feelings of shame about our bodies. But physical self-love involves embracing and appreciating our bodies, no matter their shape or size. It's essential to develop a positive body image for our overall well-being. When we cherish our bodies and treat them with respect, we cultivate a sense of self-acceptance and self-love that can positively influence every aspect of our lives.

Seeking support

It's crucial to understand that we can't do everything on our own, and it's more than okay to seek help when we need it. Whether it's confiding in a trusted friend or family member, talking to a therapist, or joining a support group, asking for help shows that we value ourselves and deserve love and support.

Self-love isn't just some trendy phrase – it's an essential practice for our mental and emotional well-being. Embracing self-compassion, taking care of our bodies, expressing our emotions, setting boundaries, finding purpose and meaning, practicing gratitude, challenging negative self-talk, forgiving ourselves, and seeking support all contribute to a loving and compassionate relationship with ourselves.

Always remember, that self-love isn't a destination but a journey that needs continuous effort and dedication. But trust me, the benefits of self-love are beyond measure and worth the investment. So, let's make self-love a daily practice, and watch as our lives blossom into something even more beautiful.

SUMMARY, ACTION STEPS & EXERCISES

- **Start a self-love journal:** Write down three things you love about yourself every day. At the end of the week, read them back to yourself and really let them sink in.
- **Practice affirmations:** Write down positive affirmations like "I am beautiful" or "I am worthy" and repeat them to yourself every morning.
- **Take yourself on a date:** Whether it's a solo trip to the movies or a cozy night in with your favorite book, take some time to treat yourself to something you love.
- **Surround yourself with positivity:** Seek out social media accounts and websites that promote self-love and positivity.

It's time to start showing yourself the love you deserve. Self-love is not selfish, and it's not a luxury - it's a necessity. By cultivating self-love, you're building a foundation for all other types of love in your life.

We talked about the importance of self-love, defining what it really means, and how it's especially crucial for black women. By loving ourselves, we are setting the foundation for all other types of love in our lives.

It's easy to get caught up in negative self-talk and internalize the negative messages we've heard growing up in a world that often doesn't see the value in black women. But it's time to challenge those thoughts and beliefs.

Coming up, we'll tackle negative self-talk and explore how it can hold us back from truly loving ourselves. Get ready, girl, because we're going to take on those negative thoughts and emerge stronger and more confident on the other side.

We'll explore how to boost our confidence and self-esteem, and I'm going to share practical tips and exercises to help you shift your mindset and break free from those limiting beliefs.

So, get excited, and let's dive into the next chapter together.

CHAPTER 2
CHALLENGING NEGATIVE SELF-TALK TO BOOST CONFIDENCE AND SELF-ESTEEM

"You are enough. You are so enough. It's unbelievable how enough you are." - Samantha Elauf

Negative self-talk is like a virus that infects your mind, your mood, and your confidence. It can sneak up on you at any moment and take over, telling you lies about yourself and your abilities.

This chapter is all about helping you to love yourself, own your power and shine bright like a diamond. As black women, we are often told to dim our light and hide our talents, but not today my friend, we are going to learn to embrace all that makes us unique and special.

I'm here to tell you, you have the power to challenge and reframe those negative thoughts and replace them with positive affirmations.

It's time to boost that confidence and self-esteem, sis!

MARCY'S JOURNEY

Marcy was a hard-working, single mother who was always on the go. She was busy working two jobs, taking care of her kids, and barely had any time for herself. However, despite all her hard work and dedication, Marcy struggled with negative self-talk and internalized oppression.

She would constantly tell herself that she wasn't good enough and that she would never succeed. Marcy felt like she was stuck in a cycle of self-doubt and fear. It wasn't until she stumbled upon exercises and practices in this book that she finally found the courage to challenge her negative self-talk.

Marcy learned how to recognize and confront her negative thoughts. She began to understand that her negative self-talk was a result of internalized oppression, and she no longer felt alone in her struggles. Marcy started to focus on self-care, and she took time for herself to relax and recharge. She even started a self-care routine that included yoga and meditation.

Marcy's journey was not easy, but with hard work and determination, she finally overcame her negative self-talk and internalized oppression. Today, Marcy is a successful businesswoman who is confident and proud of who she is. She has learned to love and accept herself, and she wants to inspire other black women to do the same.

Marcy's story is a testament to the power of self-care and emotional empowerment. You too can overcome negative self-talk and internalized oppression by understanding and challenging your thoughts. Remember, you are not alone, and you are capable of healing, growing, and thriving.

ONE OF THE BIGGEST OBSTACLES TO SELF-LOVE IS NEGATIVE SELF-TALK

Negative self-talk is the inner dialogue that we have with ourselves, and it can be very detrimental to our self-esteem and self-worth. Negative self-talk can take many forms, such as self-doubt, self-criticism, and self-blame. It can also manifest as limiting beliefs and assumptions about ourselves.

Negative self-talk can be especially harmful for black women, as we often internalize societal messages that tell us that we are not good enough or that we should be different. These messages can make it difficult for us to love and accept ourselves as we are.

So, why is it important to challenge negative self-talk? Well, negative self-talk can lead to a range of mental health issues such as anxiety, depression, and low self-esteem. It can also affect your relationships, your career, and your overall quality of life. Challenging negative self-talk can help you cultivate a more positive inner dialogue, boost your confidence, and improve your mental health.

IDENTIFYING NEGATIVE SELF-TALK

The first step to challenging negative self-talk is identifying common negative self-talk patterns. We all have different negative self-talk patterns, but some common ones include:

All or nothing thinking: This is when you see things in black or white, and there's no room for gray. For example, if you make a mistake, you think "I'm a complete failure" instead of "I made a mistake, but I'm still a valuable person."

Overgeneralization: This is when you make sweeping statements based on one or two experiences. For example, if you have a bad date, you think "I'm never going to find love" instead of "This one date didn't go well, but that doesn't mean I won't find love."

Personalization: This is when you take things personally, when they aren't even about you. For example, if your friend cancels plans, you think "They don't want to hang out with me" instead of "They might be busy or have other things going on."

Catastrophizing: This is when you jump to the worst-case scenario. For example, if you have a disagreement with your partner, you think "This is the end of our relationship" instead of "We had a disagreement, but we can work through it."

Mind-reading: This is when you assume that you know what someone else is thinking without any evidence to support it. For example, if your boss looks unhappy, you assume that they're angry with you, even if there's no reason to believe that.

Filtering: This is when you focus on the negative aspects of a situation and ignore the positive aspects. For example, if you receive a lot of positive feedback on a project, but one person criticizes it, you only focus on the criticism and ignore the praise.

Labeling: This is when you give yourself a negative label based on one mistake or trait. For example, if you forget something important, you think "I'm so forgetful and unreliable" instead of "I made a mistake, but I can learn from it and do better next time."

Should statements: This is when you have rigid expectations for yourself and others. For example, if you don't meet a deadline, you think "I should have done better" instead of "I did the best I could under the circumstances."

Blaming: This is when you blame yourself or others for things that are outside your control. For example, if it rains on the day of your outdoor event, you blame yourself for not checking the weather instead of recognizing that the weather is out of your control.

When we engage in negative self-talk, we reinforce beliefs about ourselves that are often inaccurate and unfair. We tell ourselves that we're not smart enough, not attractive enough, or not capable of achieving our dreams. These negative thoughts can become deeply ingrained in our minds, and they can become a significant obstacle to our personal growth and success.

The good news is that we can challenge and reframe these negative thoughts with practice and effort. By questioning the validity of our negative thoughts and reframing them into more positive and realistic statements, we can change the way we think about ourselves and the world around us.

CHALLENGING NEGATIVE SELF-TALK

It's important to challenge and reframe negative thoughts because they can have a significant impact on our mental health and overall well-being. Negative thoughts can create a cycle of self-doubt, low self-esteem, and anxiety that can prevent us from achieving our goals and living a fulfilling life.

One technique that can help is cognitive restructuring. Cognitive restructuring is a process that involves identifying negative thoughts, questioning their validity, and replacing them with more positive and realistic thoughts.

Let's say you have the thought "I'm never going to be successful." First, ask yourself if this thought is true. Is it really true that you're never going to be successful? Probably not. Then, ask yourself if this thought is helpful. Does this thought motivate you to act towards achieving your goals? Probably not.

Finally, reframe the negative thought into something more positive and realistic. For example, "I might face obstacles along the way, but I can overcome them and achieve success."

Evidence-based thinking

Another helpful technique for challenging negative self-talk is using evidence-based thinking. Evidence-based thinking involves looking for facts and evidence that support or contradict your negative self-talk.

For example, let's say you have the thought "I'm not smart enough to get that job." Instead of accepting this thought as true, try to find evidence that contradicts it. Maybe you have a degree in the field, or you've successfully completed similar tasks in the past. By focusing on the evidence that supports your abilities, you can challenge the negative self-talk and boost your confidence.

Practice self-compassion

It's also essential to practice self-compassion when challenging negative self-talk. Self-compassion involves treating yourself with kindness and understanding instead of judgment and criticism. When you make a mistake or experience a setback, try to respond to yourself as you would a friend. Instead of berating yourself, offer words of encouragement and support.

For example, if you make a mistake at work, instead of thinking "I'm such an idiot, I can't believe I did that," try saying to yourself, "It's okay, everyone makes mistakes. What can I learn from this experience to do better next time?" By practicing self-compassion, you can counteract the negative self-talk and build resilience.

It's also helpful to remember that you are not your thoughts. Just because you have a negative thought doesn't mean it's true or accurate. Your thoughts are influenced by many factors, including your experiences, beliefs, and emotions. By recognizing that your thoughts are not necessarily reality, you can challenge negative self-talk and create a more balanced and accurate perspective.

Positive Affirmations

Another technique that can help challenge negative self-talk is creating a list of positive affirmations. Positive affirmations are statements that help cultivate a more positive inner dialogue. These affirmations should be personal and meaningful to you.

Here is a list of powerful affirmations:

- I am worthy of love and respect.
- I am deserving of success and abundance.
- I can achieve my goals.
- I am strong and resilient.
- I am beautiful inside and out.
- I am proud of my heritage and culture.
- I am deserving of self-care and self-love.
- I trust my intuition and make decisions with confidence.
- I am a powerful force for positive change.
- I am grateful for all the blessings in my life.
- I can overcome any obstacle.
- I embrace my uniqueness and individuality.
- I am constantly learning and growing.
- I am surrounded by love and positivity.
- I am enough just as I am.
- I am deserving of love, respect, and happiness.
- I am confident in my abilities and talents.
- I am resilient and can overcome any obstacle.
- I choose to focus on my strengths and celebrate my accomplishments.

It's important to practice positive affirmations daily, especially when you're feeling down or facing challenges. Repeat these affirmations to yourself in the morning, throughout the day, and before bed. Over time, these affirmations will become ingrained in your thinking, and you'll start to believe them.

Remember, challenging negative self-talk is an ongoing process. It takes time and practice to change your thinking patterns, but it's worth it. You deserve to have a positive inner dialogue that supports and empowers you. By challenging negative self-talk and cultivating a more positive mindset, you can boost your confidence, improve your mental health, and live a happier and more fulfilling life.

So, take some time to identify your negative self-talk patterns, challenge and reframe those negative thoughts, and create a list of positive affirmations. With these techniques and a little bit of patience and perseverance, you can conquer negative self-talk and become your own biggest cheerleader. You got this!

SUMMARY, ACTION STEPS & EXERCISES

- Identify and write down your negative self-talk patterns.
- Challenge and reframe your negative thoughts using cognitive restructuring.
- Create a list of positive affirmations to replace negative self-talk.
- Practice positive self-talk on a daily basis.

It's time to give yourself a well-deserved pat on the back! Now you know all about recognizing and challenging negative self-talk. We all know that it's so easy to get caught up in those thoughts, and they can be so destructive to our self-esteem and our mental health. But, don't worry, girl, you're on the right track.

In this chapter, we talked about techniques and exercises to help you challenge and reframe those negative thoughts and replace them with positive affirmations. The power of positive thinking is real, and it can help you achieve so much in life. It's time to start believing in yourself, sis.

Remember, the journey to self-love and emotional empowerment is not an easy one, but it's worth it. And as black women, it's even more important that we take care of ourselves and build up our self-esteem. We deserve to live our best lives, and it all starts with the way we think about ourselves.

So, are you ready for the next chapter? We're going to dive into mindfulness and self-care practices. Trust me, this is where the magic happens. It's time to prioritize your mental, physical, and emotional well-being and create healthy habits that will support you in your journey of self-discovery and self-love.

I know you're busy, but taking the time to care for yourself is so important. You can't pour from an empty cup, right? So, make sure you take some time for yourself and read the next chapter. Let's do this together!

CHAPTER 3

MINDFULNESS AND SELF-CARE PRACTICES

"Take care of yourself, for when you are well, you can better care for others." - African proverb

D o you ever feel like the demands of daily life are weighing you down and leaving you feeling stressed and overwhelmed? I've been there too, and that's why I'm so excited to share with you the power of mindfulness and self-care.

As black women, we often put the needs of others before our own, but it's important to remember that we can't pour from an empty cup. Taking care of our own mental health and well-being should be a top priority, and in this chapter, we'll explore practical ways to make that happen.

We'll start by discussing the importance of mindfulness and how it can benefit our overall well-being. From there, we'll dive into easy self-care routines that you can incorporate into your daily life. You'll learn how to create a personalized self-care plan that works for you and discover the power of positive affirmations in boosting your confidence and changing your perspective.

By the end of this chapter, you'll have a solid understanding of the benefits of mindfulness and self-care, and a toolkit of practices you can use to prioritize your own mental health and well-being. And the best part? These practices are simple, practical, and easy to integrate into your daily routine.

So, grab some tea, your journal, a cozy blanket, and let's dive into this chapter together. It's time to prioritize ourselves and embrace the power of mindfulness and self-care to fuel our journey towards self-love and empowerment.

LISA'S JOURNEY TO SELF-CARE AND EMOTIONAL EMPOWERMENT

Lisa grew up in a poor, urban neighborhood, where she faced a lot of challenges, including discrimination and poverty. She internalized the negative messages she heard about herself and her community, and began to believe that she wasn't good enough, smart enough, or beautiful enough. This negative self-talk affected her mental health and well-being, causing her to feel anxious, depressed, and overwhelmed.

However, Lisa was determined to turn her life around. She was tired of feeling like a victim, and wanted to take control of her mental health. She started reading books and articles about self-care, mindfulness, and emotional empowerment, and began to practice these techniques every day.

Lisa learned how to meditate, to focus on the present moment, and to identify and challenge her negative self-talk. She also started to engage in self-care practices like exercise, journaling, and spending time with loved ones. She took time for herself and focused on her personal growth and development.

Over time, Lisa began to feel more confident and empowered. She no longer felt like a victim, and began to see herself as a strong, capable, and beautiful woman. Her negative self-talk diminished, and she was able to conquer her internalized oppression.

Lisa's story is an inspiration to all of us. She shows us that it's possible to overcome negative self-talk and internalized oppression, and that self-care and mindfulness are powerful tools for emotional empowerment. So, my dear black women, let's take Lisa's journey as a reminder to take care of ourselves and to never give up on our mental health. Together, we can conquer negative self-talk and internalized oppression, and live the lives we deserve.

MINDFULNESS AND SELF-CARE ARE ESSENTIAL FOR SELF-LOVE

I know that feeling. Your mind is always wandering, moving from one event in the past to a disappointment that is yet to happen. And you're left wondering how you can have your dream life when your mind seems to be everywhere else and not in the present.

Relax, don't beat yourself up. It is the mind's nature to stay active. But you can salvage the situation by practicing mindfulness.

Mindfulness is being present and aware of the moment without judgment. It is taking control of your now without losing focus of its significance to your future. With mindfulness, you're not trying to be a superwoman who is out to change the world at once. You're basically making the most of your life one moment at a time, one event at a time, and one lesson at a time.

MINDFULNESS PRACTICES YOU CAN DO EVERY DAY

Declutter

Not just your home but your mind as well. I know how difficult it can be to keep one's mind still and focused on the now. So, first things first. Close those tabs you've left open in your mind for too long.

You've been thinking of going to the spa, visiting a relative, taking that online course, and filing your taxes before the deadline. If you've not gotten around to doing any of them, they'll be taking up space on your mind. So, practicing mindfulness starts with completing those tasks on your mental to-do list to make room for quietness and calm in your mind.

Recognizing your emotions and paying attention to your body

When it comes to recognizing your emotions and paying attention to your body, it's important to acknowledge that societal expectations can be tough to navigate. We've been told as women to suppress our negative emotions and sometimes even made to feel bad for having them. But here's the thing: every emotion you feel has a purpose, whether it's anger, sadness, disappointment, or anything in between.

Instead of locking these emotions away or feeling like you need to be a "proper lady," try expressing them in a healthy way. You can get your anger out without insulting or hurting anyone, and you don't need to shove your emotions away either. By giving yourself permission to feel and express your emotions, you're giving yourself the opportunity to understand your wiring better.

So, don't be afraid to be different and honor your emotions. Mindfulness is all about flipping each emotion on its back and discovering why you have it, as well as how you can avoid falling into that negative emotion in the future. And remember, you're not a "b*tch" for expressing how you feel. You're human, and you deserve to be kind and respectful to yourself as you navigate your emotions.

Journaling and Gratitude

Journaling can truly be a blessing if you make it a habit. It's not just about writing down your thoughts and feelings, it's about actively reflecting on your experiences and using that reflection to learn and grow.

When you take the time to journal and stay grateful for every moment of your life, you start to notice the good things more often. It's easy to get caught up in the hustle and bustle of life and forget to appreciate what's right in front of us. But when you make gratitude a daily practice, you start to see the beauty in everything around you.

Time Management

Did you know that time management can help you stay present in the moment? I know it might not sound like the most exciting topic, but trust me, it can make a huge difference in your life. When you take control of your time, you'll be better equipped to handle things like procrastination and mental overwhelm, which can really pull you out of the present moment.

Think about it: every tick of the clock counts. When you're mindful of how you're spending your time, you can make the most of each moment and stay more aware of the present. It's not about rushing through your to-do list or cramming as much as possible into your day. It's about being intentional with your time and making sure you're spending it in a way that aligns with your priorities and values.

So, my love, start taking control of your time. Set clear goals and priorities, and schedule your day accordingly. Be mindful of how you're spending your time, and don't be afraid to adjust as needed. When you do, you'll be amazed at how much more present and engaged you'll feel in every moment.

Affirmations

We'll explore this in detail later, but let's touch on the importance of affirmations and how they can help you stay present and grounded in who you are. Affirmations are a powerful tool that can help you speak your truth and bring positive energy into your life.

When you make affirmations, you're speaking directly to yourself and telling yourself what you want to hear. This helps your mind focus on the positive and pushes negative thoughts aside. With consistent affirmations, those positive messages move from your consciousness to your subconscious, helping you stay in the present moment and enjoy all the goodness life has to offer.

For example, let's say you're about to tackle a big project at work. Negative thoughts might start to creep in, but you can quickly calm your mind with affirmations. By saying things like "I am capable of handling this project with ease" or "I have the intelligence and skills needed to succeed," you're reminding yourself of your own strength and ability to tackle challenges.

So, my love, start incorporating affirmations into your daily routine. Speak words of love, positivity, and encouragement to yourself every day. It might feel a little silly at first, but trust me, it's worth it.

Meditation

It's natural for our minds to be filled with thoughts, fears, anxieties, and plans. But the good news is that you have the power to quiet your mind and focus on the present moment.

Meditation is a powerful tool that can help you do just that. By taking just 15 minutes a day to meditate, you can reap numerous benefits for your mind, body, and soul. It's not about emptying your mind completely, but rather training your mind to focus on what is happening in the present moment.

Find a quiet, comfortable space to sit and set a timer for at least 15 minutes. Focus on your breath and let your thoughts come and go without judgment. With consistent practice, you'll start to notice the benefits of meditation in your daily life.

Self-care

Self-care is all about taking care of ourselves physically and emotionally, and it's especially important for us women who tend to be natural caregivers. We're so busy taking care of everyone else that we often forget to take care of ourselves.

But let me tell you, beautiful: you deserve some TLC too. In fact, you need it more than ever if you're taking care of other people. How can you care for others if you're not taking care of yourself first?

Self-care allows you to focus on yourself and figure out where you need a break, some fixing, or some improvement. And let's be real, mindfulness practice isn't complete if you're not nurturing yourself too. You deserve to be pampered, cared for, and spoiled rotten!

The best part is that there are so many ways to practice self-care without relying on someone else to do it for you. And these practices can also boost your confidence and build self-love.

Are you ready to dive in? Let's take some time to focus on ourselves and show ourselves the love and care we deserve.

Workout and a healthy diet

Caring for your body begins by ensuring you get all the nourishment you need from the inside out. Indulge in less junk food and opt for healthier, balanced meals. Drink plenty of water and be sure to move your muscles at least three times a week.

If you can't make time to go to the gym, you can do many no-equipment exercises at home to keep your heart healthy, and your body fit. Running around the block for one hour every other day is enough to help you stay healthy.

Social media breaks

Sometimes, all the pictures, videos, reels, and stories we view on social media clog our minds and keep us from being the best version of ourselves and dim our light.

So, sweetheart, if you find your time on Instagram and TikTok is beginning to weigh your mind down, take a break! And your body will thank you later.

Grooming

Now, I know what you're thinking - "But Jada, we all groom, what's the big deal?" Well, let me tell you, there's a lot more to grooming than just slapping on some makeup and calling it a day.

Grooming is all about taking care of yourself in a way that shows love and respect for your body. It's about nurturing every part of yourself, from your beautiful face to your hair, skin, and even your feet. When you take the time to care for yourself, you become more conscious of your body and its needs in a healthy and positive way.

So, how can you start grooming like a pro? It's simple, really. Start by establishing a daily skincare and dental routine that nourishes your body from the inside out. Take care of your hair, and don't forget to pamper your feet every once in a while.

And when it comes to clothes and makeup, wear what makes you feel confident and beautiful. There's no need to follow the latest trends or wear something just because it's "in." Wear what feels right for you, and always remember that you are beautiful just the way you are.

So, my queens, take the time to groom yourself in a way that shows love and respect for your body. When you do, you'll feel more confident, radiant, and beautiful than ever before.

Setting boundaries in relationships

I know, it may not be the most exciting topic, but trust me, it's important.

Setting healthy boundaries is one of the best ways to show that you respect and care for yourself. It's a way of saying, "I am important, and I won't let anyone treat me poorly." And when you set boundaries in your relationships, you can avoid a lot of drama that can take a toll on your physical, emotional, and mental health.

Don't be afraid to set boundaries in your relationships. Whether it's with a partner, a friend, or a family member, you deserve to be treated with respect and kindness. And if someone is not willing to respect your boundaries, then it may be time to reconsider the relationship altogether.

Remember, setting boundaries is not about being mean or unkind. It's about taking care of yourself and creating a healthy, positive relationship dynamic. So, go ahead and set those boundaries. You deserve to be happy, healthy, and respected in all your relationships.

Ample rest

When did you last have up to eight hours of uninterrupted sleep?

Resting is not laziness! And you are not a lazy woman. You are stronger than you ever imagined, and you can change the world with your ability. But you need rest! Your body needs a break from all those activities every now and then.

How can you make time for rest? Ask for all the help you need at home. You're strong, yes. But your partner can give you a hand with the chores. If your kids are up to age, they can assist too. You can ask your colleague for help with that cumbersome project. Travel, see the world, book as many spa appointments as you can afford every year, and don't be ashamed to shut down when your body needs it.

WHY SHOULD YOU PRACTICE MINDFULNESS AND SELF-CARE?

Let me tell you, there are plenty of reasons!

Here are just a few benefits you can expect:

- You can easily spot when something isn't right with your mental and physical health.
- You can beat stress and anxiety, allowing you to focus on what's important.
- You can boost your confidence and self-worth, giving you the courage to pursue your dreams.
- You can appreciate and make the most of your present, living in the moment and finding joy in the little things.

- You can discover the treasures within you, unlocking your full potential and living your best life.
- You can improve your chances of having better relationships, fostering deeper connections with the people you love.
- You can make better decisions, with clarity and purpose.

As you can see, practicing mindfulness and self-care can have a profound impact on your overall well-being. By cultivating these habits, you can improve your mental and physical health, reduce stress and anxiety, boost your confidence, and live a more present and fulfilling life. Don't underestimate the power of taking care of yourself - it can lead to better relationships, better decision-making, and ultimately, a happier and more fulfilling life.

SUMMARY, ACTION STEPS & EXERCISES

- Set aside time each day for meditation, even if it's just 10 minutes.
- Create a self-care plan and make it a non-negotiable part of your daily routine.
- Practice a simple mindfulness exercise every day, such as taking a few deep breaths or practicing gratitude.
- Start a daily journaling practice to reflect on your thoughts and emotions.
- Take a relaxing bath or indulge in a calming activity you enjoy.

We covered a lot in this chapter, from the benefits of mindfulness and self-care to simple practices you can include in your daily routine. It's important to prioritize self-care in our busy lives. By making it a part of our routine, we can enjoy the benefits of reduced stress, better mental health, and more.

Remember, self-care looks different for everyone, so find what works best for you and stick with it. Whether it is taking a walk in nature, meditating, or practicing gratitude, it's all about finding what brings you peace and making it a priority.

Let's talk about understanding and overcoming internalized oppression in the next chapter. As black women, we encounter unique challenges and messages from society that can be damaging to our self-esteem and sense of worth. But we have the power to overcome these messages and embrace our blackness with pride and confidence.

In the next chapter, we'll explore what internalized oppression is, how it can affect us, and strategies for overcoming it.

Hey girl,

I hope the book is aiding your self-empowerment journey. If so, please consider leaving a review.

Your feedback not only lets me know what resonates with you, but also helps more Black women discover the book and its transformative message.

<u>LEAVE A QUICK REVIEW</u>

US   SCAN ME   UK

Your support plays a significant role in promoting self-love and empowerment for Black women globally. Let's continue sharing the love!

With gratitude,

Jada Amari

CHAPTER 4

UNDERSTANDING AND OVERCOMING INTERNALIZED OPPRESSION

"You yourself, as much as anybody in the entire universe, deserve your love and affection." - Buddha

It's time to explore a critical issue that affects so many of us black women:

Internalized oppression.

Internalized oppression happens when we absorb the negative messages and stereotypes about our own marginalized group, making us believe those damaging ideas about ourselves. As black women, we're particularly susceptible to internalized oppression since we're constantly bombarded with negative portrayals of ourselves in the media and society at large.

In this chapter, we'll explore internalized oppression, how it impacts our mental and emotional well-being, and, most importantly, the practical steps we can take to break free from it. We'll explore the roots of internalized oppression, and the role systemic racism plays in perpetuating it. But don't worry, we won't just dwell on the problem - we'll also focus on actionable steps to conquer it.

The time has come for us to reclaim our power and live the life we truly deserve. We are worthy of feeling confident and secure in our skin, free from the burden of internalized oppression. I'm here to support you every step of the way on your journey toward self-love and acceptance.

Let's rise above!

MEET TAMEKA

Tameka was once a young, bright-eyed woman with so much potential. She had big dreams and a heart full of hope, but she soon found herself battling with negative self-talk and internalized oppression. She felt like she was stuck in a vicious cycle, with no way out. The world around her seemed to be constantly telling her that she was less than, that she would never be good enough, and that her dreams were out of reach.

But Tameka was determined to change her story. She began to understand the root of her negative self-talk and internalized oppression. She realized that it was a result of the messages she had been exposed to growing up, and that she had been internalizing these messages without even realizing it.

Tameka took a stand against her negative self-talk, and she challenged the internalized oppression that had been holding her back. She started her self-care and emotional empowerment journey, and she slowly started to see a change in herself. She began to see her worth and her potential, and she started to believe in herself again.

Tameka's journey was not an easy one, but she persevered and triumphed. Today, Tameka is a confident and empowered woman, who is living her life to the fullest and pursuing her dreams with passion and purpose. She has become an inspiration to other black women, and she is proof that it is possible to overcome internalized oppression and to heal, grow, and thrive.

Tameka's story is a reminder to us all that we are not alone in our struggles, and that we too can overcome any obstacle that comes our way. So, let's take a page out of Tameka's book and start our own journey towards self-care and emotional empowerment, so that we too can conquer negative self-talk and internalized oppression and live a life of happiness, purpose, and fulfillment.

DEFINING INTERNALIZED OPPRESSION

Let's talk about something that might be holding you back without you even realizing it. It's called internalized oppression, and it's something we as black women need to confront and heal from. But first, let's make sure we understand what it really means.

Internalized oppression is like a hidden enemy, sneaking its way into our thoughts and actions when we least expect it. It's what happens when we, as individuals who've faced discrimination or marginalization, start to believe, and live by, the negative things society tells us about ourselves. You know those awful stereotypes and false beliefs? Yeah, those. When we start to see ourselves through that distorted lens, we end up turning the oppression inward and treating those hurtful beliefs as if they were true.

Now, let me tell you, sis: if you're dealing with internalized oppression, it's not your fault. This isn't something you chose. It's a result of subconscious conditioning, where you've been exposed to certain messages and experiences so much that they start to become a part of your reality without your realization. You don't consciously hold yourself back from joy, love, and all those beautiful experiences waiting for you. But because your subconscious mind has been influenced by those negative stereotypes and experiences, you might find yourself living a life that conforms to those beliefs.

As black women, we deserve to be free from this weight, and it's essential to know that healing is possible.

EXAMPLES OF INTERNALIZED OPPRESSION

Here are some real-life examples of internalized oppression that you, as a woman of color, might be experiencing. These moments can creep up on us, and it's important to recognize them so we can start breaking free from their hold.

- You might find yourself focusing solely on domestic chores at home because society has handed you a script that says that's your role.
- Have you ever hesitated to take a leadership position, thinking that men are natural leaders, and you should just submit to their authority?
- Maybe you've felt the urge to lighten your skin to "fit in" with societal beauty standards, even though your melanin is a thing of beauty and power.
- In mixed gatherings, do you sometimes stay quiet, thinking that your "whiter sisters" have more valuable ideas or are somehow smarter than you?
- When it comes to your hair, have you chosen bone-straight extensions over your natural locks because you've been told your hair is "too nappy" or "difficult" to manage?

- Lastly, are you settling for mediocrity in your career, thinking that certain industries are just not meant for women of color?

Take a moment to reflect on your own experiences and add anything else that resonates with you.

IDENTIFYING HOW INTERNALIZED OPPRESSION CAN MANIFEST IN DAILY LIFE

It's time for a heart-to-heart about how internalized oppression might be showing up in your everyday life. You might not even realize it's happening, but it's time we bring these things to light and work on healing from them.

Ask yourself: Do you ever feel like you're not worthy of a seat at the table because of your skin color? When you're at the pool, do you feel self-conscious about being the only one with frizzy hair? Or do you get insecure when you rock your natural hair in front of a white audience?

If any of this sounds familiar, it's time to recognize that you've been listening to some harmful messages. Internalized oppression can sneak up on us in so many ways, and when we've carried these burdens for too long, we start seeing them as "normal."

Girl, you deserve so much more than just "normal." Let's shine a light on some of the ways internalized oppression might be creeping into your life, and work on healing and growing together.

Negative self-talk

Sweetheart, we've all heard hurtful things about our race, and it takes a lot of strength not to internalize those words and repeat them to ourselves. Internalized oppression often shows up as negative self-talk, and it doesn't just stop at echoing what's been said to us. We might find ourselves using our own experiences to reinforce those harmful beliefs and even predicting our future based on them.

But we're not going to let those thoughts control us anymore, honey. Together, we'll challenge them and kick them to the curb.

Feeling like you don't belong

Have you ever felt like an outsider because of your race? Whether it was being called the 'n' word as a child or feeling like you must change your appearance to fit in, internalized oppression can make us hyper-aware of our differences. But we're going to rise above those feelings and embrace our unique beauty and power as black women.

Holding onto negative stereotypes

Have you ever heard of the "angry black woman" stereotype? It's a hurtful myth that black women are ill-tempered, sassy, and hostile. Sometimes, we're fed this image so much that we start to believe it and act it out. But together, we'll break free from those limiting social scripts and become the unstoppable women we were meant to be.

Limiting Beliefs

Let's be real, love. We've all had moments where we felt like we weren't smart or capable enough to face certain situations. It's okay to have moments of doubt, but when we continuously dismiss our potential for greatness because of negative labels, that's internalized oppression at work.

These limiting beliefs can create glass ceilings that hold us back from achieving our dreams. But we're going to shatter those ceilings and step into our power as black women.

TECHNIQUES TO OVERCOME INTERNALIZED OPPRESSION

It's time to stop being your own oppressor, darling. You can't let those negative beliefs weigh you down any longer. We're going to work together to unlearn and overcome internalized oppression with these techniques: Unlearning Negative Beliefs

I know it can be tough to face those negative beliefs that have been holding you back and kick them out of your life for good; but remember, I'm right here with you, cheering you on and believing in the incredible woman you are.

Let's tackle those beliefs one at a time. Find a cozy spot to sit, and let your hands, legs, and face relax. Close your eyes if it helps, and take three deep, cleansing breaths. When you're ready, open your eyes and begin writing down the limiting beliefs you've held about yourself – those thoughts about your body, mind, and emotions that have kept you from shining.

As you write each belief, take another deep breath and exhale, imagining that toxic mindset leaving your mind with each breath. Beside each belief, jot down the experiences that led to that belief and how you've unintentionally reinforced it.

You might think, "Jada, I can't believe I ever thought that way about myself." But, darling, there's no shame here. These beliefs didn't come from you; they were forced upon you. We're identifying them so we can say goodbye for good.

Together, we'll uncover thoughts like:

- "I'll never reach the top of my career because I'm a black woman." Maybe you've seen your black female relatives struggle in their careers because of their race. And now, despite your hard work, no one seems to notice your contributions.

- "Nobody loves me, so I need to keep everyone at a distance." We've all felt that way at some point, right? Life throws us curveballs, leaving us with scars that make us hesitant to let others in. So, we build these walls around ourselves, thinking it's the best way to stay safe. But what if I told you that these walls are holding us back from the love and connection we truly crave? Sometimes, our emotional armor, once our shield, turns into a barrier that keeps us from forming genuine, heartfelt bonds.

Take your time. Write down all the negative beliefs you can remember and let them out.

It might not be easy. You may feel emotional or even shed some tears. But know that by doing this, you're releasing those harmful beliefs from your mind. You're doing an amazing job, and I'm so proud of you!

Reframing Negative Thoughts

Now that you've untangled yourself from those limiting beliefs, let's reshape your thoughts to prevent them from creeping back in.

Nip Negative Thoughts in the Bud

Whenever negativity hovers, swat it away, and don't allow it to make a home in your mind. Be vigilant, darling. Seemingly innocent observations can transform into destructive patterns if left unchecked. Thoughts like "She just got the job because she's white" might ignite a raging inferno of internalized negativity.

Look at the Big Picture

Rise above the negativity by focusing on the positives in your life, regardless of your race. How can you do this? Remind yourself of your accomplishments and the goodness around you. A gratitude journal can be a powerful tool to keep your sights on the blessings.

When doubt whispers that you'll never get that promotion because no black woman has ever advanced in your field, remember your intelligence and determination landed you the job in the first place. When your mind tries to convince you that black women don't experience lasting love, cherish the affection from your family, spouse, and children.

Express Yourself

It's your time to shine. Let your voice ring out. You are wise, vibrant, and brimming with life-changing ideas. Don't hold back for fear of judgment or rejection. The world needs your unique perspective and gifts.

Defy the odds, be the solution to problems around you, and watch those old beliefs crumble away, leaving you empowered and unstoppable.

Surrounding Yourself with Positive Influences

You've finally cleared out all that negative self-talk and limiting beliefs! But don't let that space in your mind sit empty, or else those pesky thoughts might just sneak back in. Here's what you need to do:

- Shower yourself with positive words! Speak affirmations daily. They might not click right away, but trust me, they'll work wonders eventually.

- Remember all the beautiful blessings in your life - your loved ones, your accomplishments, everything! Pro tip: set a picture of your faves as your phone's screensaver. Every time you pick it up, you'll be reminded of how blessed you are.
- Protect your energy, queen. If your subtly racist neighbor drains you, it's okay to keep your distance.
- Let nature's positivity seep into your soul. Go for a beach stroll or chill in your backyard, soaking up the birdsong.

And if progress feels slow, remember this: it took years, maybe even decades, to internalize that negativity. Be gentle with yourself and trust the process.

Practicing Self-Care and Self-Compassion

Life isn't always sunshine and rainbows, right? Sometimes things get tough, and it's during those moments that negative thoughts and internalized oppression can creep in. That's when we need to show ourselves some serious love and kindness.

It's time to practice self-compassion and indulge in self-care. Treat yourself with the same understanding and gentleness you'd offer to a friend. Nourish your body, pamper your hair, and strut your stuff with confidence, because you deserve it!

No more entertaining those harmful beliefs or allowing societal expectations to hold you back. It's time to evict those negative thoughts from your mind and embrace the amazing person you are. You've got this, and together, we'll rise above the challenges and come out stronger than ever.

SUMMARY, ACTION STEPS & EXERCISES

- Use journal prompts to identify negative beliefs and where they came from.
- Practice self-compassion exercises, such as giving yourself grace and forgiveness.
- Identify positive influences in your life and try to surround yourself with them.

In this chapter we discussed a very important topic, internalized oppression. This is when we have internalized negative messages and beliefs about ourselves that are perpetuated by society's expectations and systemic racism. I talked about how this can manifest in daily life and gave you some techniques to help you overcome it. It's essential that we identify and challenge these harmful beliefs so that we can move forward with confidence and self-love.

Remember, you are not alone in this struggle. So many of us have faced and continue to face the effects of internalized oppression. But we can break free from those chains and embrace our true selves. I hope that this chapter has helped you understand the impact of internalized oppression and how to overcome it.

Now, let's move on to the next chapter where we'll talk about healing from trauma and past wounds. We all carry our own baggage from past experiences, and it's important that we address and work through that pain to move forward. I'm here to guide you through this process and help you discover your inner strength and resilience. So, let's keep pushing forward, sis. The journey to self-love and emotional empowerment continues!

CHAPTER 5
HEALING FROM TRAUMA AND PAST WOUNDS

"Your past does not define you, but it shapes you." - John N. Mitchell

Are you struggling with the pain of past experiences?

Girl, it's time to prioritize your healing.

As black women, we often carry the weight of past traumas, whether it be from experiences of racism and discrimination or from past relationships. But it's okay to seek help and healing from these wounds. In this chapter, we'll discuss the impact of trauma on our mental health and techniques for healing, including the importance of seeking professional help.

I know this can be a tough topic to talk about, but it's so important, especially for our mental and emotional well-being. Trauma can leave deep emotional scars that affect our self-esteem and self-worth, which is why it's crucial to acknowledge and process our past experiences.

The focus of this chapter is learning about different tools and techniques for healing. We'll also discuss how to create a self-care routine that prioritizes your mental and emotional well-being, so you can move forward with strength and resilience.

You'll also have a better understanding of how trauma and past wounds can affect self-love and how to begin the healing process. You'll also learn the importance of self-compassion and self-forgiveness in the healing journey.

Remember, healing is a journey, not a destination. Take it one day at a time and know that you're not alone. You got this!

UNDERSTANDING TRAUMA AND ITS IMPACT ON MENTAL HEALTH

When you hear the word trauma, what pops into your head? Maybe it's one of these:

- Loss of a loved one
- Sexual abuse or assault
- Physical abuse or domestic violence
- War and terrorism
- Emotional abuse or separation
- Neglect and bullying
- Stigmatization and racism
- Internalized oppression
- Accidents or natural disasters
- Betrayal or breach of trust

Trauma is our response to negative experiences like these. It's how we react to events we find distressing, even when others might not understand our pain. When you're traumatized, your body can experience stress during, immediately after, or even long after the incident.

How we process trauma varies depending on factors like the nature of the event, our past experiences, and our emotional makeup.

The Effects of Trauma

Trauma doesn't just hurt, honey; it can wreak havoc on your body, mind, and soul. Left untreated, it can lead to other health issues. Sadly, trauma impacts are all too common among black women, often untreated because we've been conditioned to deny our need for mental health care.

How trauma affects the body

We sometimes assume that non-physical trauma does not necessarily affect our physiological makeup. This assumption is untrue and may also be why most trauma survivors do not get thorough treatment.

Trauma affects the brain (and the physical state of different body parts) in many ways. These impacts include physical exhaustion, panic attacks, uncontrollable muscle movements, headaches, nausea, sleep and eating disorders, substance abuse, and organ failure in severe cases.

How trauma affects the Mind

Research has found that trauma survivors have their brains rewired to focus more on survival and regulation than cognition (as with the average brain). This is why a traumatized person easily suffers anxiety, depression, irritability, mood swings, and concentration problems.

Trauma can also cause a person to experience hopelessness, loss of self-esteem and self-worth, and unnecessary suspicions.

Post-Traumatic Stress Disorder (PTSD)

PTSD is a severe behavioral and mental disorder that people develop from unmanaged exposure to traumatic events.

Sadly, PTSD is usually a prolonged episode of trauma that can further aggravate trauma symptoms.

How do you know you have PTSD?

- Having nightmares or disturbing flashbacks of the traumatic event.
- Getting emotionally or physically distressed at the slightest reminder of the event.
- Avoiding places, people, or activities that bring up memories of the event.
- Becoming hypersensitive and quickly alerted or frightened.
- Having little or no control over your emotions or actions.
- Resorting to self-destructive habits to numb the pain or memory of the event.
- Losing hold of positive emotions or losing interest in things that once appealed to you.
- Having a hard time keeping up with all your relationships.

I will not say I understand what you're going through. That would be flagrantly unkind of me – whether I've ever had to deal with trauma. I did not experience the exact thing you went through, and I may be unable to decipher how hard it's been for you.

But I am pretty sure of one thing: you can experience healing and a complete release from your emotional, physical, and mental wounds. You can get disentangled from the web of trauma that has kept you from showing up as your best.

Yes, love, your days can be bright and colorful, filled with hope and fervor. So in the following few pages, we will look into different techniques to help you heal from trauma.

I can also give you my unequivocal assurance that these techniques work. But beyond following the processes, I need you to tap into your rich supply of strength and lavishly release your hope for healing. Trust me, these techniques would be grossly ineffectual without the overflow of healing energy coming within your being.

TECHNIQUES FOR HEALING FROM TRAUMA

Trauma-Focused therapy

Yes, sis. It is what you are thinking. We need to make peace with the past and revisit (with the help of a professional) the cause of our trauma to completely heal from it.

If we avoid the traumatic event, we'd only end up treating symptoms and numbing pain, which never stops until our minds can no longer regurgitate the pain and hurt from the causative incident.

Unfortunately, numbing the emotional pain associated with trauma also stands in the way of accurately diagnosing the condition. While you can always shove down the pain, guilt, shame, or anger and lead a pretty average (although grossly unhappy) life, you may never come around to see reasons to deal with the root cause – until things get completely out of hand.

So, if you're dealing with PTSD from harrowing experiences like a car accident, the death of a loved one, abuse, and separation, professional help that allows you to digest and get over the traumatic event can help you heal.

Symptom-Based Treatments

Symptom-based trauma healing technique focuses on alleviating PTSD symptoms to initiate healing. It focuses on how your current situation (thoughts, emotions, and physical symptoms) is linked to the bad experiences of the past.

Like I did the first time I came across this healing technique, you may wonder, "why not deal with the roots, and the branches will die off?"

Well, you may have symptoms that are linked to trauma and not know it – especially when the traumatic event isn't considered a big deal in your society. By studying and treating your symptoms, your therapist can better locate the cause of the trauma to help you heal.

Mindfulness and Self-care Practices

Mindfulness and self-care practices like meditation and journaling can help you manage trauma and its devastating effects. Mindfulness techniques like grounding can help you connect to the present and empower you to take control of your situation.

However, it is best to use meditation to heal from trauma when you have the support of a professional. For one thing, sitting calmly during meditation can lead you to relive the terrible experience. And without the right help, you may drown in the negative emotions, and regress into survival mode.

Forgiveness

I know, sis. Forgiveness almost always never comes that easy. It's hard to forgive that man who stole your life to satisfy his lustful feelings. It's nearly impossible to release the careless driver whose car crushed your parents' future on the highway. And other times, you can't get over the guilt of not doing enough to prevent a traumatic incident.

But, YOU'VE GOT TO LET GO.

When you forgive the people (including yourself) who caused your predicament, you release yourself from the grip of negative emotions and energies that can impede your healing. That means you'll be making more room for positivity and light – essential indicators of effective healing.

But don't get me wrong here, darling. Forgiveness does not mean suppressing your feelings or ignoring trauma symptoms. You can honestly express how you feel, acknowledge the consequences of the incident, but also forgive and let go.

IMPORTANCE OF SEEKING PROFESSIONAL HELP FOR TRAUMA HEALING

As black women, the "superwoman syndrome" often makes us believe it is not okay to show off our weaknesses. We're told to "keep your troubles in the closet and show up as the strong, relentless woman you are," even when trauma impacts are crushing us from within.

But I do not want you to be that woman who denies herself an opportunity to completely heal from trauma because she wants to "stick it out alone to show how strong she is."

When you're going through a hard time, you need all the help you can get. And that includes embracing professional service for trauma healing.

Three common ways you can seek professional help when healing from trauma are explained below:

Seeing a Therapist

Seeing a therapist (or psychologist) has long been labeled "something for people with mental disorders," especially among people of color.

But nothing could be further from the truth.

While a therapist may not be a certified medical professional, they can help you heal from trauma in the following ways:

A therapist is experienced in utilizing various healing techniques and can progressively help you through your trauma, as they may have had to do for others. So, their expertise gives you a better shot at healing than when you decide to heal on your own.

A therapist can also help you see the bigger picture in your healing process. This means that they can identify and help you get rid of addictions and disorders you developed due to the trauma. A therapist will also listen to you, validate your feelings, and help you see where you're missing without undoing a nerve.

Consulting a Psychiatrist

A psychiatrist is a medical professional with relevant medical qualifications specializing in mental health.

When you experience trauma that affects your brain and its function, it is only ideal to see a psychiatrist for proper diagnosis and treatment. That is because your brain is like every other organ in your body and can also be affected by trauma. When that happens, you will need the help of a qualified medical practitioner for proper treatment.

More reasons a psychiatrist is an important figure in your healing from trauma include:

A psychiatrist can evaluate, diagnose, and treat any physiological symptoms that may arise from your trauma.

A psychiatrist can prescribe medications for your symptoms and monitor the progress of your physical and mental healing from trauma.

They can also provide psychological therapy to help you achieve wholeness.

Joining a Support group

The old saying, "no man is an island, no man lives alone," couldn't be any more valid. Humans need relationships with other people to thrive – even while dealing with traumatic stress.

Some people shy away from support groups because they would rather not have everyone know what they're dealing with. Honestly, if you believe seeing a therapist is enough for you, that's fine.

But a support group is vital for thorough healing from trauma for the following reasons:

- Support groups give you a sense of community, reassuring you that you aren't alone in your troubles. You get the comfort that your symptoms and trauma responses are expected and have nothing to do with your natural makeup. This understanding can help hasten your healing.
- Support groups provide a safe and encouraging environment where you can freely share your experiences and receive support and encouragement from others.
- Support groups can offer you a great deal of human connection, which is always a beneficial inclusion to trauma and PTSD treatments.

- Joining a support group will help you deal with isolation, which is a significant trigger of depression, anxiety, and suicidal thoughts.
- When you join a support group, you have access to helpful systems, resources, and information to help you handle daily challenges with your condition. And the good thing is that these resources have helped someone else heal from a similar situation.
- It is easier to stop addictions you developed from trauma when someone else knows about them. And being in a support group means you can freely talk about your addictions without judgment.

You don't deserve to have suffered that heartbreaking experience – nobody should ever have to go through that. But you also do not need to suffer its impacts all your life.

It is okay to be a "strong black woman" and still recognize that you need to heal from the impacts of the hard stuff you've gone through.

Healing may not come easy, but I can assure you that it is within the realm of possibility, and you can have it in full.

So, get up, get all the help you need, and pull through that experience!

You can do it!

SUMMARY, ACTION STEPS & EXERCISES

- Reflect on past experiences that may have caused trauma and how they continue to impact your mental and emotional health.
- Start incorporating self-care practices into your daily routine, such as journaling, meditation, or exercise.
- Consider seeking professional help if you're struggling to manage the impact of past trauma on your mental and emotional health.

This chapter was all about healing from trauma and past wounds, which can be a difficult but important process for our mental and emotional well-being. We discussed what trauma is and how it can affect our mental health and well-being, as well as techniques for healing from trauma, such as seeking professional help and practicing self-care. We also talked about the importance of creating a supportive environment and taking care of ourselves as we heal from trauma.

Remember, healing is a journey, and there's no one-size-fits-all approach. It's important to be patient and compassionate with ourselves and seek the support we need to navigate the healing process.

Now, let's turn our attention to building, navigating, and maintaining healthy relationships, which is vital to our overall well-being. In the next chapter, we'll talk about the importance of healthy relationships, what healthy relationships look like, and how to cultivate and maintain them in our lives. So, let's keep going and continue on this journey towards healing, growth, and empowerment!

CHAPTER 6

BUILDING, NAVIGATING, AND MAINTAINING HEALTHY RELATIONSHIPS

"A true friend is someone who sees the pain in your eyes while everyone else believes the smile on your face." - Unknown

'm excited to explore building, navigating, and maintaining healthy relationships, which are key components of self-care and mental wellness.

As black women, societal expectations and negativity can impact our relationships. But this chapter is going to help you understand what makes a relationship healthy and how to develop the skills needed to make it work.

Firstly, you'll learn why taking care of yourself first is crucial in any relationship. By focusing on your own mental and emotional health, you'll be better equipped to deal with the ups and downs of relationships. We'll also talk about the importance of setting boundaries and expectations in relationships. You'll learn how to communicate your boundaries and expectations to your partner, and how to deal with those who don't respect them.

Communication is key in any relationship, and we'll talk about the importance of open and honest communication, navigating disagreements, and the importance of compromise. By the end of this chapter, you will have a better understanding of how relationships can impact self-love, and the importance of healthy relationships.

You will also have the tools to recognize and avoid toxic relationships, set boundaries, communicate effectively, and build and maintain healthy relationships with those around you.

Remember, the relationships we have with others can greatly impact our self-esteem, well-being, and self-worth. It's important to surround ourselves with people who support and uplift us, rather than those who tear us down. So get excited, you're about to discover how to empower yourself in your relationships!

DEFINING HEALTHY RELATIONSHIPS

Darling, you are deserving of the absolute best from people – even when society tries to convince you otherwise because of your beautiful skin color. You are worthy of peace and joy in all your interactions because you, my dear, are a blessing to this world. No lies here. Now, you might be asking, "Why are my relationships such a hot mess?" The truth, sweetheart, is that merely starting a relationship isn't enough to reap the rewards of a great connection. Relationships can only be beautiful and fulfilling when they are healthy and nurturing. So, what does a healthy relationship look like? Well, beyond good intentions, healthy relationships are characterized by essential values like mutual respect, communication, trust, support, and security. Let's quickly dive into these virtues.

Mutual Respect

As simple as it may sound, mutual respect stems from a deep understanding that you are unique, and so is the other person. Embracing this understanding allows you to make peace with your differences in perspective, views, paradigms, and beliefs. It's perfectly okay for them to be themselves, and for you to be you, while your relationship continues to thrive. When this understanding exists in your relationships, you can confidently say that mutual respect is present.

Communication

We are social beings, so we are often energized simply by interacting with other people. However, productive interactions can only begin when there is a communication of desire, want, and information between two or more people.

If you cannot clearly communicate with people, how do you establish a relationship with them?

Furthermore, you'll agree with me that nobody can read another's mind. So, proper communication not only helps you understand the people you are in a relationship with, it also reduces the risk of conflicts, disagreements, and a clash of interests.

Trust

You wouldn't want to have a relationship with someone who doesn't trust you, would you?

While trust develops in stages and intensities, your relationship will flourish more effectively when a robust degree of trust is established.

It's okay to give people the benefit of the doubt and trust them until they give you a reason not to. And when they do, you need to redraw the lines in that relationship.

Growth

Relationships have lives too. In the same way we can stop growing when we are not adequately fed; relationships die when we do not make deliberate efforts to improve them. So, a conscious decision and effort to improve makes relationships healthier.

NAVIGATING CONFLICTS AND DISAGREEMENTS IN RELATIONSHIPS

Conflicts are never a peachy experience – especially when we are hurting. But the truth is that human interactions cannot do without conflicts.

Why?

No two people in the world are the same. And when you interact with other people, you also interact with their different backgrounds, cultures, education, beliefs, and values, which in most cases, will differ significantly from yours. Consequently, conflicts, misunderstandings, and disagreements are bound to arise.

But how you handle conflicts will determine their effects on your relationships.

In this age, we're constantly told to throw away anything that distresses us or costs us our peace of mind.

Your peace of mind should be a priority, no doubt about that. But will you destroy all your relationships at the slightest provocation? Because conflicts will arise in every one of them.

You don't deserve to be void of thriving relationships. Being the queen you are, you were not designed to navigate life in loneliness.

So, when conflicts arise, instead of opening the trash can, there are numerous ways you can approach and resolve things to preserve and improve your relationship.

Have a positive Perspective

One quick question for you – how do you approach conflict? Take some time to think about that.

Do you see conflict and misunderstanding as warfare and a time to show the other party how tough and unbending you are? Or, do you find conflicts as opportunities to understand your individual makeup while embracing the differences?

When conflicts and misunderstandings arise in your relationships, you can salvage things by seeing the conflicts as an opportunity to hear the other person out and understand what's important to them.

The truth is that the conversation of values, preferences, and priorities may never come up in some relationships until there is a disagreement. Wouldn't it be better to see a disagreement as an opportunity to communicate individual preferences and values?

Let's be real, your relationships may not be that bad after all. You just need to start viewing conflicts from a friendlier and more dynamic perspective.

Dialog Some More – Without Emotions

Have you noticed how smooth problem-solving can be in relationships when everyone communicates openly and honestly? Often, a few moments of respectful conversation can douse the flames of conflict.

To resolve issues amicably, make sure to share your feelings and expectations. If emotions are running high, it's okay to take a step back and let the other person know you'll revisit the topic later.

Once you're calm, kindly express how you felt hurt and suggest ways to avoid future conflicts.

Remember to offer the other person a chance to share their thoughts too. You might be mistaken, or there could be room for compromise. By listening, you might learn valuable lessons that will help your relationship thrive in the long run.

Acceptance Mindset

When conflicts pop up in relationships, it may seem like the other person's dark side is trying to sabotage everything. It's tempting to lash out, but nobody's perfect. Instead of focusing on their wrongdoings, appreciate the good they bring into your life. By doing so, you'll forgive more easily and embrace their imperfections as part of their humanity.

For example, when your vivacious girlfriend gets on your nerves at a party, remember the comfort her outgoing nature has provided you. Your annoyance will dissolve, and you'll dodge a major conflict.

Though you can't always avoid conflicts, you can effectively communicate your needs to minimize misunderstandings. Check out these tips for better communication in relationships:

- If possible, express your needs and preferences verbally, and be open to hearing theirs too.
- Ensure your body language aligns with your words.
- Make your communications personal by using "I," "me," and "my" to convey your needs, not just giving commands.
- Be polite and respectful in addressing others.
- Set clear relationship boundaries.

By mastering communication, you'll strengthen your connections and navigate conflicts with grace.

SETTING BOUNDARIES IN RELATIONSHIPS

A healthy relationship thrives on mutual respect. But how do you ensure your values are honored without causing tension? It's all about setting boundaries.

When you don't establish boundaries, you risk losing control over your life, values, and identity just to maintain relationships. Worse, you might become a people-pleaser, making sacrifices for others, and questioning why your relationships aren't flourishing or your life feels chaotic despite being surrounded by amazing people.

So, remember to set boundaries to preserve your well-being and create healthier, more balanced relationships.

What Are Boundaries?

Boundaries mark where one thing ends, and another begins. In relationships, they show where your responsibility ends and the other person's starts.

Boundaries should be visible, clear, and well-communicated. They look like saying "no" without guilt when something doesn't feel right or giving your priorities space in your relationships. But remember, boundaries also mean saying "yes" and asking for help when needed. They're not walls that make you untouchable; setting boundaries doesn't mean closing yourself off.

Don't worry, boundaries aren't the enemy. They don't make you less loving, generous, or easygoing. Instead, they help you recognize your needs, protect your energy, and prioritize your well-being. Plus, they shield you from resentment, violations, and disappointments that can arise from conflicts.

Why Are Boundaries Important?

When you draw the necessary lines in your relationships, everyone gets to know their responsibilities and what they should be accountable for.

This may not sound like the best thing you've heard today, but boundaries also distribute repercussions fairly. People know what they'll reap when they express certain behaviors, reactions, and words in relationships.

Boundaries encourage mutual respect

When you install clear boundaries in your relationships, the other person will be aware of your edges. They will understand the things that unambiguously identify you and the things you are willing (and not willing) to do for the relationship. And it goes both ways.

At the end of the day, no one would have a reason to cross the line or expect the other person to act contrary to the established boundaries. In the long run, this breeds mutual respect, a vital component of every healthy relationship.

Boundaries eliminate unrealistic expectations

When you make those lines clear in your relationships, you let people know your stand. Consequently, they know what to expect from you and what not to even dream of having you do.

Making it clear that you do not jumble work with your personal life would stop your colleague from picking a fight with you when you do not open a work-related email that was sent outside work hours.

Also, emphasizing your need for solitude to your partner would ensure that they do not feel neglected when you need to shut down.

Phew!!

Boundaries keep you in good shape

Finally, when you set healthy boundaries in your relationships, you save yourself the stress of trying to be a superhero for everyone else (sorry, sis, you can't help everybody).

Do you know how huge a blessing it can be to be set free from that syndrome?

Boundaries release you from the performance pressure that comes from a false sense of shared entitlement. You won't have to feel guilty for not going that painful extra mile for someone when you clearly set out your boundaries.

Isn't that a tremendous relief?

The Different Types of Boundaries

Let's explore the various types of boundaries - physical, emotional, mental, and spiritual - so we can level up our self-care and relationships.

Physical Boundaries

Physical boundaries are the limits you set regarding your body, physical space, and belongings. It includes defining how people can touch you, invade your privacy, or use your stuff.

Broadly, physical boundaries include sexual boundaries and matters like consent and sexual preferences.

Setting physical boundaries includes letting people know they have to call you before stopping by your home. It includes extending your hand for a handshake when someone would rather have a hug.

While it's important to show love and respect to others, granting access to your emotions should be reserved for those who truly deserve it. Emotional boundaries allow you to safeguard your feelings, energy, and personal space, while also acknowledging and respecting the emotions of others.

For us as black women, setting emotional boundaries is especially crucial. We face countless challenges that can impact our emotional and mental well-being daily. So, let's explore some specific examples of how to establish and maintain healthy emotional boundaries:

1. **Clearly communicate your limits:** Be open about what you are and aren't comfortable discussing or engaging in, and don't be afraid to say "no" when necessary.
2. **Recognize and respect the boundaries of others:** Just as you want others to honor your limits, be mindful of their boundaries, too.
3. **Prioritize self-care and self-reflection:** Take time to recharge and understand your emotional needs so that you can effectively establish and maintain healthy boundaries.
4. **Surround yourself with supportive, positive people:** Seek out relationships that uplift and respect your emotional well-being.

It's perfectly okay to protect your feelings and energy by setting appropriate boundaries. You deserve to be surrounded by people who respect and honor your emotional needs.

Intellectual Boundaries

Intellectual boundaries protect your opinions, ideas, and thoughts in your relationships.

Consequently, setting intellectual boundaries means drawing that line in the sand when someone tries to belittle, criticize, or shut out your thoughts and opinions.

Intellectual boundaries also keep people from shoving their ideas and thoughts down your throat, especially when you disagree with them.

COMMUNICATING AND EFFECTIVELY ENFORCING BOUNDARIES

So, how do you address, communicate, and enforce boundaries effectively in relationships?

I know you're thinking, "Jada, won't setting boundaries make me lose my beautiful relationships?"

But I sincerely think your question should be, "Won't I remain a prisoner in my relationships if I do not set boundaries?"

So, which question would you rather deal with?

Be Clear About Your Yes and No

Don't be afraid to clearly establish yeses and nos in your relationships. You don't want to leave any room for assumptions and unnecessary excuses for violating your boundaries.

Set Up Consequences

Yes, I know. we've all been there - someone crosses our boundaries even after we've made them crystal clear. But how long will you let that continue?

The solution? Set consequences and stick to them. When people face the repercussions of crossing your boundaries, they'll realize just how much you respect yourself and your limits.

For instance, if a friend asks for a loan after being careless with money- even though you've shared your stance on financial negligence - let them experience being broke until their next paycheck. You're not being insensitive; you're protecting your mental health, asserting your own financial needs, and maybe even helping them develop better money habits. Stand your ground, and watch your boundaries become unshakable.

Control Your Exposure

Sometimes, you might struggle to set limits on others, especially if they've been stuck in their ways for years. But don't worry, it's not a dead end.

In these situations, enforce your boundaries by controlling how much time, effort, and resources you give to those who can't respect your limits. It's okay to leave a job if your boss keeps canceling your vacations or expects you to work during family time. It's okay to distance yourself from people who make hurtful comments about your beautiful 4C hair, even after you've voiced your discomfort.

Remember, being black doesn't mean you should accept disrespect from anyone, and they shouldn't disrespect you either. Stand strong and let your boundaries shine.

SUMMARY, ACTION STEPS & EXERCISES

- Take some time to reflect on what you want and need in a relationship. What are your deal breakers and what are the qualities you're looking for in a partner or friend?
- Practice active listening in your relationships. When you're having a conversation with someone, make an effort to really listen and understand their perspective without interrupting or getting defensive.
- When conflicts arise, take a step back and try to see the situation from the other person's perspective. Ask yourself what you can do to de-escalate the situation and find a resolution that works for everyone.
- Be willing to have difficult conversations with your loved ones. It's important to communicate your feelings and needs in a relationship, even if it feels uncomfortable.
- Set boundaries in your relationships. This can include things like saying no to requests that don't align with your needs, communicating your limits and needs clearly, and taking a break from relationships that are causing you stress or harm.

We explored the characteristics of healthy relationships, such as open communication, mutual respect, and support. We also discussed how to navigate conflicts and disagreements in relationships and the importance of setting boundaries to maintain healthy relationships. Remember, it's okay to prioritize your own needs and boundaries, and it's essential to have relationships that uplift and support you.

Navigating relationships can be tough, but the most important relationship is the one you have with yourself. It's time to shift our focus to our physical selves and learn to love our bodies. It can be hard in a society that values a narrow standard of beauty, but you are unique and beautiful just the way you are. In the next chapter, we'll explore body positivity and self-love, and learn how to embrace ourselves fully.

Let's take this journey of self-discovery and empowerment together, sis. You are capable of anything you set your mind to, and I'm here to support you every step of the way. Let's dive into the next chapter and learn to love ourselves inside and out.

CHAPTER 7
BODY POSITIVITY AND LOVING YOUR PHYSICAL SELF

"Our bodies are our gardens - our wills are our gardeners." - William Shakespeare

I remember the days when I struggled with body image and feeling good about myself. But that was before I learned how to embrace my curves and love my body for all its imperfections. And now, I'm sharing that knowledge with you in this chapter.

Body image and self-love are closely connected. Society's narrow definition of beauty can make it difficult for black women to love and accept our bodies as they are. That's why in this chapter, we'll dive deep into the importance of body positivity and why it's so crucial for your mental health.

First, we'll explore the roots of negative body image and how society has trained us to see certain body types as "ideal" - and how this affects our self-esteem. Then, we'll work on embracing body diversity and learning to appreciate and celebrate our bodies' unique qualities instead of comparing ourselves to others.

But we won't stop there. We'll also cover some practical tips for loving your body and feeling better about your physical appearance. You'll learn techniques to improve your self-confidence, embrace and appreciate your unique features, and celebrate the diversity of black bodies.

By the end of this chapter, you'll have a newfound appreciation for your beautiful body and the confidence to rock it with love and pride. So, let's dive in and start celebrating the beauty of our bodies!

JANINE'S JOURNEY TO BODY POSITIVITY AND SELF-LOVE

Janine, a fierce and fabulous woman, wrestled with self-doubt and the pressure of fitting into society's limited idea of beauty. But one day, she decided enough was enough and embarked on a journey to embrace her unique self.

To start, Janine made self-care her top priority. She set aside time each day for activities that made her feel good: journaling her thoughts and feelings, practicing yoga to connect with her body, and repeating daily affirmations like, "I am enough, and my body is beautiful."

Janine also built a support network, joining a body positivity group where she found other like-minded women on similar journeys. Together, they celebrated their accomplishments, shared their struggles, and uplifted one another.

To challenge her internalized negativity, Janine sought professional help. Through therapy, she learned to identify and reframe her negative thought patterns, replacing them with healthier beliefs about herself and her body.

The turning point came when Janine dared to wear a bold, colorful swimsuit to a beach outing with friends. Though anxious at first, she radiated confidence as she walked along the shore, feeling the warmth of the sun on her skin and the support of her friends cheering her on.

From that day forward, Janine cherished her unique features and stopped comparing herself to others. She inspired those around her, showing them the power of self-love and acceptance.

Janine's journey reminds us that embracing our authentic selves takes courage, support, and intentional self-care.

So, go ahead and give yourself permission to love yourself, flaws and all.

WHAT IS BODY POSITIVITY AND WHY IS IT IMPORTANT?

I need you to do one thing for me. Find yourself a mirror, and if you're comfortable, take off most of your clothing, or at least enough for you to see a good portion of your body.

Now, focus on each part of your body and notice how you feel about them. Your journal will come in handy here.

How do you feel about your hair, its texture, and its length? Are you comfortable with the shape of your face? What about your tummy, hips, and thighs?

Can you jot down the emotions that bubble up when you look at each part of your body?

Are these emotions love, happiness, acceptance, satisfaction, confusion? How about frustration? I hope not.

Now, let's talk about a term you may have heard - body positivity.

Body positivity is accepting, respecting, and loving your body, no matter its type, shape, color, or perceived flaws. As a black woman, having a positive body image means appreciating your body and its features without trying to conform to any preconceived standards of "perfection."

Unfortunately, body positivity hasn't always come easy for us black women, even though there are so many benefits to embracing a positive body image.

Let's take a quick peek at these benefits:

- Body positivity fosters unconditional self-love – you learn to love yourself wholly. It helps you appreciate your body for what it can do, rather than just what it looks like.
- Improved mental and physical health – embracing body positivity can boost your mental health and motivate you to care for your physical well-being.
- A weapon against negative stereotypes and stigmas – staying positive about your body shields you from falling victim to harmful stereotypes about black bodies.

So, let's get on this journey together and learn to love and appreciate every part of ourselves!

The Impact of Negative Body Image on Mental Health

Before we explore the effects of negative body image on mental health, let's properly diagnose how you perceive your body.

Do you feel a compulsive need to hide any part of your body from others? Are you inordinately dependent on makeup to make you look good before a public appearance? Does how you feel about your body get in the way of your work performance, relationships, and general wellbeing? Do you have an obsessive need to change something about your body? When you think about your body, do you feel a powerful hostility towards it? Have you ever described your body with a bad word?

If you nod to any of these questions, then you may be dealing with a negative body image, which can have some perilous consequences on your mental health. Let's take a look at some of them:

Decreased self-esteem and confidence

Having a negative perception of your body diminishes the worth you attach to yourself. Consequently, your confidence diminishes when you show up before others.

Anxiety and depression

Constantly dwelling on the imperfections in your body can perpetually keep you in depressive moods. It's also easy to feel anxious and entertain thoughts of self-harm when all you always see is your body's "imperfection."

Poor self-love

When you always feel like something is wrong with your body, you begin to see yourself as undeserving of love – even from yourself.

Bitterness and unhealthy comparison

Quick question. Where does negative body image come from?

Most likely from the effects of the words and actions of bullies and naysayers who supposedly had "better bodies" than we do or excessively dwelling on the seemingly perfect bodies others flaunt on social media.

When the full impact of negative body image starts to settle, you may develop bitterness towards people with "perfect" bodies, even when they're your friends or family.

Poor social habits

Because you feel "there's something wrong with your body," you'll want to keep yourself away from others. You may begin to decline invitations to social gatherings and start to withdraw from other people. You may even resort to speaking less at unavoidable meetings (at work) to avoid drawing attention to yourself.

But cheer up sugar, we'll kick negative body image in the butt in a few moments. You'll surely receive the freedom you need to be who you are unapologetically!

TECHNIQUES TO DEVELOP A POSITIVE BODY IMAGE

When we say, "Yay! I accept my body, despite society's expectations and stereotypes about what a body should look like," we still acknowledge those social scripts somewhere in the back of our minds. And, when society pushes us, we might find ourselves slipping back into those old thought patterns and hating our bodies again.

So, can we go a step further than just "accepting" our bodies? How about truly loving our bodies unconditionally?

When you love your body wholeheartedly, you stop caring about what society thinks a black woman's body should look like. Instead, your body becomes the center of your world, and it's the only body that matters.

But how can you reach this point?

Start by detaching your self-worth from any perceived bodily "flaws."

Ask yourself, does your skin color stop you from being an amazing mom, a good friend, or a dedicated employee? Does the shape of your nose, which you might not be fond of, make you any less of a loving, patient, or hospitable woman?

Think about it, sis. Those so-called "flaws" that society throws in our faces don't affect our capabilities, do they?

If they don't, it's time to detach our sense of worth from how we think our bodies look and instead focus on the impact we make in the world. Embrace your unique beauty and remember that you are so much more than your appearance. You, my dear, are truly incredible.

Be Grateful for what your body does

I know loving our bodies may not be as easy as it sounds. But instead of isolating your hip dips and hating on them, see your entire hips as a vital part of being able to walk, dance, and carry your body weight.

Making a list of the great things your body helps and allows you to do every day will help you stay grateful for the gift of your body.

Love your body as the only body in the world

Imagine if there was only a single $100 bill in the world. How could you tell if it was fake (bad) or authentic (good)? You wouldn't be able to, right?

Similarly, there's no real standard for differentiating a "good" body from a "bad" one – until you start looking at other people's bodies and making those harmful comparisons.

So instead of getting caught up in comparing yourself to others, embrace and cherish your body like it's the only one that exists. Celebrate its uniqueness and appreciate it for all the incredible things it does for you every day.

Why not start by turning a blind eye to what you see on social media and fashion magazines? Love your body, because it's the only one you've got!

Explore your body's glory

Maybe you started hating your body when you were the only one not getting your ballet positions correctly in ballet school. You felt you couldn't get ballet right because something must be wrong with your body.

But I bet you don't know what wonders your body can do besides dancing. The only way to find out is to explore!

Learn something new, visit new places, and meet new people. They can help you discover hidden beauties in your body!

Take care of your body

I can bet that the celebrity with the hourglass figure and glass skin against whom you compare yourself may not have been born that way. They must have invested time and money to get their bodies that way.

Take care of your body, girl. You won't know when you fall head-over-heels in love with it, cellulite, hip dip, and all.

Put health over looks

Our obsession with the number on the scale makes staying positive about our bodies even harder. Instead of waiting until you weigh 120 pounds to love your body, why not focus on keeping your body healthy? That's more than enough to help you appreciate your body and take your attention off "imperfections."

Eat balanced meals, work out for at least 150 minutes every week, get enough rest, and seek medical help whenever you notice something isn't right.

Lend a hand

When you make life better for someone else, you won't believe the intensity of fulfillment that can come from that. As you're giving yourself a high five for putting a smile on someone else's face, you'll definitely not tell your tummy "not to enjoy the accolades because they won't stay flat and tight."

Focus on Your Strengths and Redefine Beauty

Instead of letting external opinions define our worth, let's focus on our strengths and achievements. We all have unique talents and abilities, so why not invest in those and cultivate our own definition of beauty?

It's true that even some of the most successful women have faced insecurities, but recognizing our accomplishments and focusing on our passions can empower us to redefine beauty on our terms. When we excel in our chosen fields and take pride in our skills, we can begin to shift our self-perception and embrace our own brand of beauty.

Let's celebrate our brilliance, determination, and resilience because beauty isn't just about appearances – it's about the strength and grace we embody as we navigate this world and make a difference in our own lives and the lives of others.

Speak to yourself

Affirmations, girl!

They are super helpful in reconditioning your thoughts and feelings about your body. Always remind yourself that "your body is not the problem" and that "you are worth more than the number on your scale."

Speak to someone

If these techniques do not help you develop a positive body image, you may need to see a professional. A therapist can use cognitive behavioral therapy, medication, or physical fitness therapy to help you step away from the negative feelings you have about your body.

THE IMPORTANCE OF CELEBRATING THE DIVERSITY OF BLACK BODIES

We've been there, haven't we, honey? Staring at the magazines, the billboards, the TV screens, and seeing one type of 'beauty' glorified, one that often doesn't look like us. We've felt the sting when our natural hair is labeled as 'unprofessional,' or when our skin tone isn't represented in the makeup aisle. We've held our breath, sucked in our bellies, and tried to fit into molds not meant for us.

But let's get one thing straight, black is beautiful. We are beautiful. Our bodies, whether they are petite or curvy, whether our skin is ebony or café au lait, whether our hair coils tightly or flows in waves, are all part of the beautiful spectrum of black womanhood.

Think about our sister Serena Williams, with her strong, athletic body, defying the norms of a tennis world that never made space for her. And yet, she made that space, didn't she? She showed us all that strength is beauty.

Or consider Lupita Nyong'o, her dark skin glowing, her short hair defying gravity. She redefined Hollywood's beauty standards, reminding us that dark skin is not just beautiful, it's worthy of admiration and celebration.

And let's not forget about our sister Lizzo, who uses her platform to remind us that our bodies are perfect just as they are. She's out here, unapologetically herself, reminding us all that confidence and self-love are the most attractive qualities a woman can have.

When we embrace our diversity, when we honor the different shades, shapes, and textures that make us who we are, we break away from the stereotypes that have kept us in chains. We free ourselves from the body image struggles that have been holding us back. We make it easier for our sisters to love themselves without an ounce of shame, to unleash their potential without any reservations.

And just imagine the power of that, sisters. Imagine a world where every black woman knows her worth, where she sees her beauty reflected back at her, not just in the mirror, but in the world around her. That's the world we can create when we celebrate the diversity of black bodies. That's the world we deserve. So, let's start today, right now. Let's celebrate ourselves, in all our diverse, beautiful glory.

SUMMARY, ACTION STEPS & EXERCISES

- Write down three things you love about your body and read them every day.
- Practice self-love by taking time to care for your body, such as through exercise, a relaxing bath, or getting a massage.
- Surround yourself with positive influences by following body-positive accounts on social media and unfollowing accounts that make you feel bad about your body.
- Start a gratitude journal where you write down things you are grateful for about your body.

It's essential to love ourselves from head to toe, inside and out. In this chapter, we explored body positivity and its importance for our mental health. We delved into techniques for developing a positive body image, embracing our individuality, and celebrating the diversity of black bodies. Remember, you are beautiful, and your body is unique, deserving of love and care.

Now, let's move on to the next chapter, where we'll focus on financial empowerment and self-sufficiency. We'll discuss the significance of financial independence and how to build a stable financial future. We'll talk about budgeting, managing debt, and creating savings plans that work for you. Sis, it's time to take control of your finances and work towards achieving your goals.

CHAPTER 8
FINANCIAL EMPOWERMENT AND SELF-SUFFICIENCY

"Wealth is not about having a lot of money, it's about having a lot of options." - Chris Rock

Hey sis, are you ready to take control of your finances and become self-sufficient?

Money, oh money.

It's one of those topics that can make us feel uneasy, but it's so important for our mental and emotional health. That's why we're going to dive into the nitty-gritty of financial empowerment and self-sufficiency. With the right mindset and a solid plan, you can take control of your finances and live the life you deserve. Financial stability and independence can greatly impact our self-love and overall well-being.

In this chapter, we'll dive into financial literacy, goal setting, budgeting, and wealth building to help you thrive financially.

Soon you'll have a better understanding of how to achieve financial empowerment and self-sufficiency. You'll also have tools and strategies to create and stick to a budget, save and invest for the future, and recognize and address financial toxicities. So, grab your notebook and a pen, and let's get to it!

SHANAE'S STORY

Shanae found herself in a difficult situation, stuck in a dead-end job, living paycheck to paycheck, and swamped by debt. It felt like she was barely keeping her head above water. But with determination, she turned her life around, becoming a shining example of financial empowerment and self-sufficiency for her community.

To regain control of her finances, Shanae developed a detailed budget, carefully tracking her income and expenses. She pinpointed areas where she could cut back, like eating out less and canceling unused subscriptions. She also identified opportunities to increase her income by taking on freelance gigs, negotiating a raise at work, and exploring side hustles. With unwavering dedication and grit, Shanae paid off her debt and started building her savings, even setting up an emergency fund for unexpected expenses.

But Shanae's transformation went beyond money. She prioritized her mental and emotional well-being by setting aside time for self-care activities, such as meditation, journaling, and exercising. She joined a support group to help her work through internalized oppression and negative self-talk, and she learned to set healthy boundaries in her relationships. As a result, she became a more assertive and confident woman, unafraid to ask for what she deserved.

Today, Shanae is a thriving business owner, nurturing a supportive community of women she empowers and uplifts. She stands as a testament to what's possible when we take charge of our finances, mental health, and lives.

Shanae's story reminds us that no matter how challenging our circumstances, it's never too late to create change. By taking control of our finances and nurturing our mental and emotional well-being, we can become the powerful, self-sufficient, and unstoppable black women we were meant to be.

EMBRACING MONEY MATTERS FOR BLACK WOMEN

As much as we're easily tempted to dismiss money matters as something meant for men, there's no denying that money is a critical aspect of our lives. And no, there is nothing too complex about money that our brains cannot comprehend!

If having or not having money can critically affect your life, don't you think being in control of your money would change your life for the best? Now, that is what financial empowerment and self-sufficiency are about.

According to a *Fortune* article, black women are the highest participants in the U.S. labor market. Yet, research shows that we earn $11,752 less than the average American each year. Why's that?

More of our kind need to be financially empowered – first with the proper knowledge and attitude about money.

When we are financially empowered and self-sufficient, we fortify ourselves to properly negotiate the outcomes of our lives without overly depending on "men." A financially empowered woman will undoubtedly have a healthy sense of self, healthy relationships, and a better shot at a beautiful, drama-free life.

However, financial empowerment only begins when we recognize and have the correct beliefs about money and see it as a tool to help us lead the kind of life we truly want – as black women.

TIPS FOR BUDGETING AND SAVING MONEY

You're a smart, beautiful, and hardworking woman. You give your best at your job or business, doing your best to meet your needs and those of your family.

But do you always get to that shadowy point where you wonder where all your money goes?

If you work 9-5, do you always end up broke before your next paycheck?

Self-sufficiency cannot be achieved if a few days after you get paid you start wondering what happened to the money.

If you don't always know "where all the money went," you don't have control of your finances. And if that is the case, you may never come around to get lasting and profitable stuff done with your hard-earned bucks.

There's a solution to this problem - budgeting.

Budgeting can be a vital tool for attaining financial independence, and here is how:

Budgeting sets a vision for your money

Picture this, honey: Budgeting as your personal financial GPS, guiding you to make those savvy decisions about how to work your hard-earned coins. No need for fancy finance officer-level details – just a well-crafted plan to help you allocate your funds right where they need to go. With a clear vision for your cash flow, you'll be in control and ready to make the most of every dollar.

Budgeting gives you control over your money

Money is essential to our survival, and it would be advantageous to us if we could exert some level of control over how it is used. Budgeting gives you that control. And when you master the right way to control your budget, you've begun your journey to financial empowerment and independence.

It helps you identify wealth-leakers

When you draw up a budget and follow it through, you'll be surprised at the unnecessary things that have been swallowing your money.

Budgeting encourages savings

With a carefully drawn budget, you'll always have a rough estimate of what you can save comfortably each month. And if you really put in the time and discipline to follow your budget, taking out some savings will be a lot easier than when you spend indiscriminately.

Budgeting motivates you to improve your earnings

Budgeting gives you a meaningful estimate of the impact of your current earning. It highlights if your paycheck can only cover the bills, groceries, and one or two hospital treatments after insurance or if it gives you enough room for other expenses. You know, like treating yourself to books and courses every month. Sounds pretty good, right?

Your budget gives you facts with which you can make significant decisions

A consistent budgeting pattern should immediately tell you if spending summer in Hawaii will be possible or not.

Now, you're ready to budget your income.

Here's the most critical budgeting tip:

What are the things you **need;** what are the things you **want?**

Someone now feels like, "Come on Jada, don't we already know those?"

Yes, we do.

But, how well do you remember this difference when your girlfriend sends you the link to hair extensions on buy-two-get-one-free sales? How well do you distinguish your needs from your wants when that seemingly harmless window shopping becomes an unplanned shopping spree?

Not much, I guess.

When we can draw a distinct line between our needs and wants, budgeting – and sticking to a budget – shouldn't be as challenging as it sounds.

What happens after I differentiate my needs from my wants?

Ensure that your income covers all your needs at the time (including debts, savings, and investments) before even a single want is attended to.

Ensure your budget is real enough

It's easy to get high on the "budgeting and discipline" thing that we forget to make our budgets realistic. At the end of the day, we're disappointed that we cannot stick to our budgets.

To create a realistic budget, get and use a rough estimate of your monthly expenses by looking at what you've spent in previous months even if you did not use a budget. Look at your bank and credit card statements for more accurate details. Now, use those numbers or slightly less to draw your budget.

Stay accountable

Spending beyond your budget might feel like a harmless indulgence, but keeping yourself in check is the key to financial success. With an accountability partner or a handy app, you'll feel motivated to stick to your budget like the queen you are.

What are the best ways to save?

To ensure that you save consistently and efficiently, always save a specific percentage of your income. But don't be hard on yourself; remember that every month will be different. Also, dedicate each savings account to a specific purpose so you're not tempted to use it for something trivial.

BUILDING FINANCIAL INDEPENDENCE AND SECURITY THROUGH INVESTMENT AND ENTREPRENEURSHIP

Budgeting and saving are tremendously important tools you can use to manage your money. They also help you achieve your financial goals.

But you'll agree that no matter how good one's budgeting and saving skills may be, true, lasting, and progressive financial independence will only happen when your income continues to be greater than your expenses. And truth be told, you'll always have more things to pay for with each passing day. That means your income needs to constantly rise.

What I'm saying is that one way to improve your financial independence and security is by increasing your earnings. And there are several ways to increase your earnings, even when that pay raise isn't happening as fast as you want.

Clear debt that sucks your funds through interest

Yes, sis. Interests on debts can be detrimental to your financial independence plan if you do not figure them out early.

The first thing you need to do to secure your financial future is to clear off those debts. Doesn't a credit card sound like the best place to start?

Multiply your money through investments

Often, black women overlook the idea of monetary investments because we either believe they're too complicated or we fail to deal with the fear of parting with large sums of money and prefer to be safe than sorry.

Whatever it may be for you, I need you to know that investments are literally the way to "multiply" your money. Thankfully, there are so many channels that help us multiply money today.

Real estate

Either with buildings or pieces of land, you can multiply your money in real estate by going into house hacking, property wholesaling, or joining real estate investment groups or trusts.

401(k) Matching

Not many people know this, but you can gain an additional 50% of the amount in your 401(k) retirement account if your employer offers matching funds.

Equities and bonds

If your risk appetite is on the lower side, you can delve into low-risk investments like equity, bonds, and trusts.

Stock exchange

Quickly compound your investment interest by buying and trading in different stock portfolios. News has it that on average, the stock market churns out a whopping 8% yearly return.

Now, it must be stated that I am not a financial advisor, nor do I play one on TV. But from my own personal experience, these give you an idea of different potential ways to diversify your money.

WEAR THE ENTREPRENEUR'S CAP

Thankfully, starting a business is no longer the big deal it used to be for black women. Plus, there are now so many categories you can work on to become financially independent without quitting your job immediately.

Some practical steps to starting your own business

- Think of a problem you want to solve. And no, I'm not saying you have to deal with the pollution problem in your country. How about creating something that helps busy moms prepare meals faster? Or something that gives people the wisdom they need for survival in the workplace?
- Map out your audience by doing something I call customer profiling. Who are your potential customers? What do they want the most? Where do they live? How old are they?
- Come up with a strategy around how your business helps your customers.
- How will your customers reach you? Online or on-site?
- Define your business structure and legal framework.
- Register with the IRS, the government, and other relevant institutions.

- Get a space and stay visible - online, in a store, or from your home.

What if you already have a full-time job and the extra full-time of being a mom and a wife?

Running your own business is still possible, but in your case, you may have to place more demand on people and passion.

People

There are different ways you can leverage people to build and run a successful business even when you are not ready to quit your job. First, you may need people to run part or the entire business while you are at work. You will also need to up your networking game to help you reach more customers.

Passion

Not precisely the emotional attachment we place on things. Here, I mean something you're really good at and enjoy doing because passion is grit. So, what is that one thing you do effortlessly? Speaking to teenagers? Creative creations?

Your side business needs to be something you have the expertise to do easily so you do not overextend yourself.

Investing in YOU

Let's dive deeper into the most crucial investment you can make as a black woman - investing in YOU. Most successful people share one thing in common: a resilient mindset and attitude that keeps them pushing forward, even when facing adversity and setbacks. But, remember that nobody's born with that mindset - it's something that's nurtured and cultivated through personal development and self-education.

Continue to build your library with mind-expanding books like this one, seek the guidance of a knowledgeable coach, follow a mentor who inspires you, and never stop taking self-development courses. Each of these investments in yourself will pay lifelong dividends, untouchable by market crashes or policy changes. You'll be nurturing your resilience and inner strength.

By investing in your personal development, not only will your attitude towards money and success flourish, but you'll also be better equipped to handle life's challenges. You'll find it easier to set and achieve goals, maintain healthy relationships, and build the financial independence you've always wanted.

Embrace personal development and make it a top priority. You'll see a transformation in every aspect of your life, including your financial well-being. Remember, you are your most valuable asset, and investing in yourself is the key to unlocking the abundant life you deserve.

SUMMARY, ACTION STEPS & EXERCISES

- Set financial goals and create a budget that reflects your priorities and values.
- Start tracking your expenses and find areas where you can cut costs.
- Consider investing in stocks, bonds, and real estate to build long-term financial security.
- Research and explore entrepreneurship opportunities that align with your passions and interests.

Financial empowerment and self-sufficiency are crucial to achieving our goals and living our best lives. In this chapter, we discussed why it's essential to take control of our finances and shared practical tips for budgeting, saving money, and building financial independence and security. By prioritizing financial wellness, we can reduce stress and anxiety, and focus on pursuing our dreams. Remember, you are worthy of financial freedom and stability.

As we wrap up this chapter, let's reflect on the valuable insights you've gained and commit to implementing these tips in your financial life. And as you continue on your self-care journey, let's move on to the next chapter, where we'll discuss prioritizing self-love in the workplace; because you deserve to feel appreciated, respected, and fulfilled in your professional life.

Let's thrive in every aspect of our lives, sis!

CHAPTER 9
PRIORITIZING SELF-LOVE IN THE WORKPLACE

"Success is liking yourself, liking what you do, and liking how you do it." - Maya Angelou

Hey sis, have you ever stopped to think about how we often put our self-care on the back burner in the workplace? We're so focused on breaking through those glass ceilings, proving our worth, and climbing the corporate ladder that we forget to take care of ourselves along the way.

It can be a tough balancing act to meet work demands while prioritizing our self-care, but it's crucial for our well-being. That's why in this chapter, we'll talk about the challenges we face and techniques we can use to set boundaries, build a self-care routine around work demands, and prioritize our self-love in the workplace.

I can hear you thinking, "But Jada, I already have so much on my plate, how can I possibly make time for self-care?" Believe me, I get it. Making changes like these can be daunting, especially in a work environment. But trust me, it's worth it.

In the pages ahead, we're going to look at the importance of self-care in the workplace. When we make our own well-being a priority and take care of ourselves, amazing things can happen. We can create the lives and careers that we deserve, filled with purpose, happiness, fulfillment, and overall well-being. So let's get to it and start prioritizing self-love in the workplace!

THE IMPORTANCE OF SELF-CARE IN THE WORKPLACE

As black women, we are industrious, passion-driven, and relentless in achieving our goals – including targets at the workplace. And yes, we want our bosses and colleagues to see how much value we bring to the table.

So, we begin the life-sapping endeavor of trying to show up with our superwoman cape at work. We give our best to assigned tasks and are willing to take on more than we can comfortably handle. And we always have a broad smile plastered on our faces as we nod to more work than necessary.

People finally notice how hardworking we are. But that's not all they see. They also notice how much of a hero we can be – for them too. They dump their responsibilities on us by asking for small favors that gradually alchemize into full-blown workload transfer. At this point, guilt zips our mouths shut, and the fear of taking off our superhero cloak stops us from protesting.

In no time, our work performance starts to decline because our focus is divided. We begin to work extra hours more often or even take additional work home. We're burnt out, always exhausted, and even get sick. We no longer have time to spend with family, partners, and friends or to focus on our personal growth.

Soon we no longer have anything to contribute to work meetings, and our relationships with coworkers and supervisors start to decline. We even begin to resent the people whose "burdens" have become too heavy for us.

When we realize we've been carrying someone else's burden, we may decide to continue carrying the burden to keep up with the superwoman show, start to look for a new job, or risk having a "toxic" work environment when we finally break free and confront our prison warden.

Unfortunately, all this drama could have been avoided if only we understood that we could prioritize self-love and still be – and remain – the best employee of the month.

Yes, darling. Self-love needs to be expressed everywhere, including the workplace, whether you run your own business or work for someone.

Here are a few reasons self-love should never be up for negotiation at the workplace.

Self-love keeps you from taking responsibility for other people's work

It's okay to lend a hand at work. But don't you have a coworker who always has requests like "can you help me pick up X file from Y company since they're closer to your home?" or "can you help me deal with this during lunch because I have a meeting at that time?"

Practicing self-love in your work keeps you from constantly doing other people's work and getting overextended. If you can make it clear that you appreciate yourself, your time, and your energy, which is self-love, nobody will ask for "tiny favors" that steal you away from your responsibilities.

You work smarter and are more productive when you exercise self-love at work

Self-love in the workplace creates a cycle, but it's up to you to decide which cycle it will be – virtuous or vicious?

When you prioritize your time and energy and let your coworkers and bosses see how much you do, you won't squeeze in more than your share of work into your 8-hour work day. You can then focus on your responsibilities, give them your best shot, and be more productive.

You enjoy better health

Imagine that you skip lunch in a bid to saddle your responsibility with that of someone else's at work. That's one meal down.

By the time you get home, you only have enough energy to get out of your work clothes and sprawl on the bed. But you're hungry, so you make do with junk or salt-laden takeout. You do this five times a week, and after a few months, your health starts to protest the malnutrition and lack of proper rest.

Better work-life balance

If you have a family, spending time with them during the week may be impossible. And by the weekend, you're juggling catching up with the girls, spending time with your partner and children, cleaning up your home, and doing the week's laundry.

At this point, you may start to hate your job because "it doesn't allow you time for other important things in your life."

But when you can exercise self-love at work, you'll be able to properly balance work with your personal life.

Better chances at a juicier pay

When practicing self-love helps you focus on your responsibilities at work, you can always negotiate for higher pay when your results are visible and impactful.

You'll have access to better networks

You don't think so, right? How can we access better career networks when we keep telling everyone what "not to do" around us?

Truth is, when you set healthy boundaries at work, it makes your relationships with coworkers easier and drama-free. Plus, you'll start to attract people with similar attitudes – who are most likely successful.

Self-love increases your confidence at your workplace

Self-love does not only show up when we need to defend ourselves from ill-treatment at work. In fact, it begins with us respecting and honoring ourselves enough to put in the necessary work to make us valuable at the workplace. When we do so, we become indisputably confident in our abilities.

COMMON CHALLENGES TO PRIORITIZING SELF-LOVE IN THE WORKPLACE

We love and appreciate ourselves so much that we want everyone to understand this, but exercising self-love at work may not be the easiest thing to do because of the following reasons.

Pressure to please others

Of course, you value yourself. You even used a dozen affirmations this morning to reassure yourself of your self-worth. But because you cannot say no to your office bestie or even dare to offend your line manager, you "happily" take on more than you can chew.

An irrational desire for recognition and promotion

It's that time of the year when promotions are dished out, and the "employee of the month" selection is around the corner.

So, it's easy to convince ourselves that there is no time to prioritize anything else until you land that promotion or at least "get high enough on the career ladder."

Unreasonable bosses and coworkers

Some employers should be in jail for how hard they push their employees. And, let me tell you, there's no denying that some of these coworkers can be straight-up inconsiderate in how they operate in the workplace. Understandably, these kinds of people can make it challenging to exercise any form of self-love or priority for personal well-being at work.

More than enough criticism in the workplace

Practicing self-love can be tricky when you're in a work environment where your deliverables are constantly criticized, even before they are reviewed.

TECHNIQUES FOR SETTING BOUNDARIES AND SAYING "NO"

The most effective way to express self-love at work is to set reasonable boundaries in your interactions.

The following techniques will help you set healthy workplace boundaries and say no when necessary - without having your heart in your mouth.

Understand your boundaries first

Before setting any boundaries, you need to understand what is okay for you and what isn't. You need to have an excellent grasp of your capabilities and thresholds to confidently say no when people try to cross your limits.

Put yourself first

People can call it selfish, self-centered, or "ethically inappropriate," but one way to draw that line in the sand at your workplace is by considering your time and wellbeing before appending your signature to any contract or agreeing to any deal. Does it resonate with your values? Or will consenting to this means you will no longer be able to prepare dinner for your family every other day?

Babe, the worst that can happen is getting fired from your job, which may eventually happen if you fail to set those boundaries.

Always refer to your employment contract

Girl, I feel you. It can be tough to stand up to your boss or put a coworker in their place. But remember, you're an employee, not a company servant.

Here's the deal, sis. Always keep your employment contract in mind. When you need to make a stand, ensure it aligns with what's written in that agreement. If it does, don't be afraid to bring up those clauses in your conversations. You got this!

Be vocal about it

It is dangerous to assume that everyone at work knows they ought to respect your time, opinion, energy, and preferences. It is your responsibility to make that clear. As much as possible, air your concerns via email and during staff meetings. And be sure to let someone know when they're toeing across your boundaries.

Tread the overtime lane wisely

Working overtime to meet up a tight schedule can quickly translate to a sheer display of a lack of self-love. So, you may want to embrace overtime with great caution, even if you're getting compensated for it.

A perfect example would be if you are always assigned a workload that is too much for you to complete within stipulated timelines. Learning to ask for more time will help you draw a nice line around how your time should be demanded at work. Or better yet, you can ask to delay non-urgent tasks.

Do it fast

Let me share some wisdom from Rachel Hollis's book, "Girl, Stop Apologizing." When it comes to setting boundaries, you only need to address it once. Give your response – even if it's a tough "no" – right away when someone tries to cross your boundaries. This way, you won't get stuck with those "maybes" and "let's sees" that end up committing you to something that's not a priority. Stand firm.

Reduce your exposure to toxic people

Maybe you have a manager who can be negatively critical of your work. The straightforward way to deal with such an attitude is to give them no reason to "criticize" your work. And oftentimes, part of that "no reason" would be to either work more than you should or spend more time on a task than is required.

Unfortunately, even the perfected work may still not please the person. The way out? Ignore such attitudes. Do your job excellently and pay no attention to unnecessary criticism. You may also need to let go of trying to get this person's approval. Else, you may put yourself up to be controlled. Even better, never take their words to heart so you don't cross your boundaries to prove them wrong.

HOW TO CREATE A SELF-CARE ROUTINE AROUND WORK DEMANDS

If you're thinking, "Haven't we already dealt with self-care in the previous chapters?"

My answer is, yes, we have. But I really need us to see that self-care doesn't only happen when you follow a morning face-care routine or when you decide to sleep in during the weekend.

You can also extend your self-care routine at your workplace, even when work demands your life. Here are a few things to continue to make priorities in your life.

Sleep properly

Have a regular sleep routine that refreshes you for a productive workday.

Be excellent

Let's be honest. The quality of work you turn in is about the most significant measure of how much love you have for yourself. So, do you want to show that you're worthy of respect? Set a standard of excellence for yourself at work, and never go below it.

Practice punctuality

Not just to escape unwanted deductions from your paycheck. Punctuality is a clear indicator that you genuinely respect your time.

Toot your horn

Sweetheart, people are too busy trying to figure out their own lives to boast about your achievements for you. And I know society will say it is "modest" to allow others to sing your praises. But having healthy self-love means you know you deserve those accolades, and you want others to see what you've achieved. Who knows, you could be setting yourself up for an excellent recommendation.

Take lunch breaks – and sick leaves too

If your employment contract allows you some days every month for sick leave, use them to the last minute – even if you never get sick. And if you're about to feel guilty about using sick leave when you're not ill, think about your period.

Isn't that enough reason to get two days off from the stress at work? And for my ladies who have outgrown this bleeding stage, it's okay to just say, "I need a break."

Be unreachable after work hours

If it means having your work phone number separate from your personal number, go for it!

Also, make a habit of not opening work emails after work. You don't want to be called at 9pm to send a file – unless you hold a medical position, and need to save a life urgently.

Engage in hobbies outside work

Nothing nourishes the soul more than leaving the work-laden workplace and getting home to joyfully immerse yourself in something that brings you great delight.

This hobby could be regular exercises before or after work, a side hustle, writing, Netflix and chill, or time with your family.

Nurture your other relationships

When other relationships in your life are active and well-connected, you will have less need to seek solace and sympathy from your workplace. Unfortunately, expecting too many personal benefits from a work environment is one of the leading causes of workplace conflicts and toxicity.

Keep your emotions formal

You're angry? Express it. But through an ethically friendly email instead of verbal name-calling.

Remember, self-care at work isn't just some fancy buzzword they throw around in corporate meetings. It's about rolling up your sleeves and putting in that work to ensure your well-being and productivity are in sync. We're talking about walking that fine line, the one that balances your professional grind with your personal peace. And when we find that sweet spot, that's where the magic happens, that's where we find a work-life blend that doesn't just exist but thrives!

SUMMARY, ACTION STEPS & EXERCISES

- Journal about the ways you can set boundaries at work.
- Make a list of activities that help you relax and de-stress after a long workday.
- Create a self-care routine that works for you by setting small goals to incorporate self-care into your workday.
- Practice saying "no" to tasks that don't align with your values, goals, or personal boundaries.

Prioritizing self-love in the workplace can be challenging, but it's essential for our mental and emotional health. Remember that you are worthy and deserving of respect, and it's okay to set boundaries and say no when necessary. Building a self-care routine around work demands can help us feel more in control and better equipped to handle stress.

Now that we've discussed prioritizing self-love in the workplace, it's time to focus on building a support system. In the next chapter, we'll explore the importance of having a support system and how to cultivate healthy relationships with friends and family. Remember, you don't have to go through life alone. Let's dive into the next chapter and learn how to build a network of support!

CHAPTER 10
BUILDING A SUPPORT SYSTEM

"A single rose can be my garden...a single friend, my world." - Leo Buscaglia

I n this chapter, we'll be discussing the importance of having a support system in place for your mental health. We all need support, and as black women, we often jump over many hurdles, making a support system a necessity. We'll talk about identifying the supportive people in your life and how to build a support system that works for you.

We'll explore techniques for finding support, from joining support groups to connecting with a trusted therapist.

First things first, let's acknowledge that building a support system is not always easy. It takes time and effort to cultivate healthy relationships, and it can be especially challenging if you've experienced trauma or other difficulties in your life.

But remember, you are worth it, and having a strong support system can make all the difference in your mental health and overall well-being.

So grab a pen and paper and let's get started! Building a support system is the foundation for emotional empowerment and we're in this together!

JANELLE'S JOURNEY: FROM ISOLATION TO EMPOWERMENT

I have to tell you about Janelle. She was a strong black woman, but she was feeling like life's challenges were just too much to handle on her own. Overwhelmed and lonely, she knew she needed a change. That's when she discovered the power of building a support system - her very own sisterhood.

Janelle decided it was time to stop going it alone, so she took the first steps to create her own support network. She hit up old friends, started going to a support group for black women, and connected with others who shared similar experiences on social media.

As Janelle's squad grew, her mental health started to shift. She felt less alone and more connected to a community that genuinely had her back. This newfound support system gave her encouragement, accountability, and a sense of belonging.

Now, listen to this: Janelle and her squad had weekly check-ins where they'd share their highs and lows, along with their personal strategies for overcoming obstacles. They practiced mindfulness techniques, like deep breathing exercises and progressive muscle relaxation, to help handle stress and anxiety. The group also held workshops on assertiveness training, where they learned to communicate their needs and boundaries like the queens they are.

They even planned monthly self-care days, doing things like group meditation, journaling sessions, or weekend getaways to recharge their minds and spirits. They created vision boards to visualize their goals and dreams, and they held each other accountable for making moves towards those dreams.

Janelle's story shows us the power of a strong support system on our emotional well-being. By surrounding ourselves with uplifting, encouraging, and accountable sisters, we can tackle negative self-talk and internalized oppression head-on, allowing us to heal, grow, and thrive.

So, take a page from Janelle's book and remember that we don't have to face life's challenges alone. Building a support system is essential for our emotional well-being, so don't be afraid to reach out and create connections. You deserve to feel empowered and in control of your life, just like Janelle, girl!

IMPORTANCE OF HAVING A SUPPORTIVE NETWORK

I used to believe that I could do it all on my own. I was ambitious, driven, and had a clear vision of what I wanted to achieve. I thought that if I just worked hard enough, I could achieve my dreams and create the life I wanted for myself and my family. But as time went on, I began to realize the importance of having a supportive network.

It wasn't until I hit a rough patch in my life that I truly understood the power of a support system. I had just started my own business, and I was struggling to make ends meet. I felt like I was in over my head, and I didn't know how to ask for help. I was afraid of appearing weak or incompetent.

But one day, I decided to reach out to a few of my close friends, who were also black women entrepreneurs. I opened up to them about my struggles and asked for their advice and support. To my surprise, they were incredibly supportive and understanding.

They shared their own stories of struggle and offered me guidance and encouragement.

It was then that I realized the importance of having a supportive network. I saw firsthand how it could make all the difference in the world. I began to identify and build a support system, which included not just my friends but also my family, colleagues, and mentors.

I started attending networking events and joining professional organizations, which gave me access to a wider community of like-minded individuals. I also made an effort to nurture my relationships with the people in my life, checking in on them regularly and offering support whenever I could.

With my support system in place, I was able to accelerate my progress. I found that having people in my corner who believed in me and my dreams gave me the confidence and motivation to keep pushing forward, even when things got tough. They reminded me of my strengths, cheered me on during my successes, and helped me navigate the challenges that inevitably came my way.

Now, as I reflect on my journey, I am grateful for the support system I have built. It has been instrumental in helping me achieve my dreams and thrive and grow. And as I continue to grow and evolve, I know that I can count on my network to be there for me, every step of the way.

As you can see, having a supportive network is a crucial component in your empowerment journey. Your support system can provide you with motivation, guidance, and accountability, all of which are essential to achieving your goals. Let's expand on each of these topics.

Encouragement and Motivation

A supportive network can provide you with encouragement and motivation, especially during challenging times. They can remind you of your strengths, help you overcome obstacles, and cheer you on when you need it most. Having people in your corner who believe in you and your goals can be a powerful source of motivation.

"When I'm feeling discouraged, I turn to my best friend for encouragement. She always reminds me of my strengths and lifts me up when I need it."

Accountability

Your support system can also hold you accountable for your actions and decisions. They can check in on your progress, offer feedback, and help you stay on track. When you have people who are invested in your success, it's easier to stay accountable and focused on your goals.

"My accountability partner checks in with me regularly to see how I'm progressing towards my goals. Knowing that I have to report back to her keeps me on track and focused."

Guidance and Advice

Having a supportive network can also provide you with guidance and advice. They can offer insight, share their experiences, and help you navigate challenges. Your support system can be a valuable source of knowledge and expertise, helping you make informed decisions and avoid potential pitfalls.

"My mentor has been instrumental in helping me navigate the ups and downs in my life. She provides me with valuable guidance and advice that I wouldn't have access to otherwise."

Networking Opportunities

Your support system can also provide you with networking opportunities. They can introduce you to people who may be able to help you, provide you with leads, and offer referrals. Your support system can help you expand your network and create new opportunities.

"Through my support system, I was introduced to a successful entrepreneur who has become a mentor and friend. I never would have met him if not for my network."

IDENTIFYING AND BUILDING A SUPPORT SYSTEM

Identifying and building a support system is an essential aspect of achieving your goals. Having a support system can help you stay motivated, overcome challenges, and stay on track towards your desired outcome. In this section, we'll discuss different techniques you can use to identify and build your support system.

Reaching Out to Family and Friends

Your family and friends are the people who know you best and can provide you with the emotional support you need to achieve your goals. Reaching out to your loved ones and sharing your goals with them can help you stay accountable and motivated. They can also provide you with encouragement, advice, and a fresh perspective.

"I reached out to my cousin and shared my goals with her. She has been my biggest supporter and encourages me when I feel like giving up."

Seeking Out Mentors

Mentors are individuals who have already achieved what you are striving towards and can provide you with guidance, advice, and motivation. Seeking out a mentor can help you gain valuable insights and knowledge that can help you achieve your goals more efficiently.

"I reached out to a successful businesswoman who I admire and asked her to be my mentor. She has provided me with valuable advice and insights that have helped me navigate the business world."

Joining a Support Group

Joining a support group can provide you with a sense of community and shared experience. Being surrounded by individuals who are working towards similar goals can help you stay motivated, share advice and resources, and overcome challenges together.

"I joined a support group for writers and have found it to be incredibly helpful. Being surrounded by other writers who understand the creative process has helped me stay motivated and committed to my writing goals."

Hiring a Coach

Hiring a coach can provide you with personalized support and guidance that is tailored to your specific needs and goals. A coach can help you stay accountable, identify your strengths and weaknesses, and provide you with strategies to overcome obstacles.

"I hired a health coach to help me achieve my fitness goals. She has provided me with personalized guidance and has helped me stay on track towards my desired outcome."

USE YOUR SUPPORT SYSTEM TO ACCELERATE YOUR GOALS

You know, having a support system is crucial when it comes to achieving your dreams. A support system consists of people who uplift, motivate, and inspire you to be your best self. These individuals believe in you, cheer you on, and hold you accountable for your goals.

Here are some techniques for using your support system to accelerate your goals:

Share Your Goals

Share your goals with your support system. This can include your friends, family, mentors, or a coach. By sharing your goals, you hold yourself accountable and create a sense of responsibility to follow through with them. Your support system can also offer words of encouragement and motivation when you need it most.

"I shared my goal of starting a business with my mentor, and she was able to offer guidance and advice on how to get started. She also held me accountable by checking in on my progress regularly."

Seek Guidance

Don't be afraid to seek guidance from your support system when you feel lost or stuck. Your support system can offer a different perspective and provide insights that you may not have considered. They can also offer practical advice on how to overcome any challenges you may be facing.

"When I was struggling with a major decision in my life, I turned to my best friend for guidance. She was able to help me see things from a different perspective and offered some practical advice that helped me make the right decision."

Celebrate Your Wins

When you achieve a goal, celebrate it with your support system. This not only provides a sense of accomplishment, but it also helps to reinforce the belief that you can achieve your dreams. Your support system can offer words of encouragement and celebrate with you, which can boost your motivation and help you stay on track.

"When I finally launched my business, I celebrated with my family and friends. Their support and encouragement made the accomplishment even more meaningful, and it motivated me to keep pushing forward."

Surround Yourself with Positivity

Surround yourself with positive people who uplift and encourage you. Your support system should be made up of individuals who believe in you and your dreams, and who support you through thick and thin. By surrounding yourself with positivity, you can maintain a positive mindset, which is essential for growth.

"I make a conscious effort to surround myself with positive people who believe in me and my dreams. Their support and encouragement keep me motivated and focused on my goals."

Using your support system to accelerate achieving your goals is essential for success. By sharing your goals, seeking guidance, celebrating your wins, and surrounding yourself with positivity, you can stay accountable, motivated, and focused on achieving your dreams.

SUMMARY, ACTION STEPS & EXERCISES

- Make a list of people in your life who provide you with support and decide to connect with them regularly.
- Consider joining a support group or seeking out a therapist to provide professional support.
- Practice being vulnerable and open with the people in your support system to deepen those relationships.
- Set up regular check-ins with your support system to stay accountable and motivated.

We've come to the end of the chapter, where we covered the importance of building a supportive network and how it can help accelerate achieving your goals and dreams. I hope this chapter has shown you the power of having a support system and given you some techniques for identifying and building one.

As black women, we often feel like we have to do everything alone, but that's just not true. Building a support system can help you stay accountable, motivated, and give you a different perspective.

We discussed how to identify people who will support your goals, how to communicate your needs with your support system, and how to leverage your network to help accelerate your dreams.

Now, it's time to take what you've learned and apply it in your life. Reach out to people in your life who you know will be supportive of your journey to growth and self-empowerment. Start building a network of people who can help you stay accountable, provide motivation, and give you a different perspective on your journey.

Now that we've discussed how to build a support system, let's move on to our next chapter, where we'll talk about something near and dear to our hearts - celebrating and embracing our blackness.

I can't wait to dive in with you and explore what it means to be proud of who we are, inside and out.

CHAPTER 11
CELEBRATING AND EMBRACING OUR BLACKNESS

"Black is beautiful." - Unknown

It's time to celebrate and embrace our beautiful blackness! In this chapter, we'll discuss the challenges of being a black woman in society and how to build pride and confidence in our black identity. Together, we'll learn techniques for embracing and celebrating black culture and identity.

We'll dive into navigating the challenges of colorism, discrimination, and stereotypes that affect us as black women. I know it's not always easy, but we have to build a strong sense of self-love and self-worth to combat these challenges. We'll also explore the unique aspects of black culture, like our hair, music, and food, and how these cultural elements help shape our identity.

Learning to love and embrace our blackness is a crucial step towards healing and empowering ourselves. We'll discuss techniques for building pride and confidence in our black identity and how to take control of our narrative. Sis, we are more than our skin color or stereotypes. We are strong, beautiful, and powerful black women!

So let's get ready to celebrate and embrace our blackness! We are beautiful, powerful, and amazing, and it's time we started owning it.

KALISHA: A STORY OF EMBRACING BLACKNESS AND TRANSFORMING HER LIFE

Kalisha was just like many of us, struggling with negative self-talk and internalized oppression. She felt like she was never enough and always compared herself to others. But one day, Kalisha decided enough was enough. She was done living in fear and self-doubt and decided to embrace her blackness wholeheartedly.

Kalisha started by celebrating the unique qualities and traits that made her, her. She acknowledged her heritage and all that her ancestors had endured to get her where she was today. This newfound appreciation of her blackness was liberating for Kalisha. She began to see the beauty in her skin color, hair texture, and everything else that made her different.

Kalisha also started to surround herself with positive, uplifting, and supportive people who celebrated her for who she was. This allowed her to feel empowered and confident in her own skin. She started to speak up for herself and became more assertive in her personal and professional life.

As Kalisha continued to embrace her blackness, she noticed that her life was transforming. She felt more fulfilled and happier, and her self-esteem and confidence skyrocketed. She realized that self-care and emotional empowerment were key components of her journey to healing, growth, and thriving.

Kalisha's story is a testament to the power of embracing our blackness and taking care of our mental health. We are all worthy and deserving of love, respect, and happiness, and it all starts with loving and embracing ourselves just as we are.

UNDERSTANDING THE IMPORTANCE OF CELEBRATING AND EMBRACING YOUR BLACKNESS

Embracing and celebrating our blackness might feel like swimming against the current, especially with society always trying to hold us back. Even internalized oppression can be a hurdle in recognizing our true selves. But let me tell you, there's nothing more important than embracing and celebrating our identity as black women.

Solidifies your confidence in the black race

When you celebrate your black identity, it strengthens your confidence in your roots. It gives you a sense of belonging and pride in a community that has overcome unbelievable challenges and come out stronger.

Boosts your self-image

Embracing your blackness means you're at peace with everything that makes you a black woman, and you love it all. No more worrying about the size of your nose or the shape of your waist. That, my love, is the essence of a healthy self-image.

You encourage other black women

Imagine where we'd be if trailblazers like Oprah Winfrey, Viola Davis, Michelle Obama, and Gabrielle Union hid from their black identity. Yeah, shining a spotlight on our blackness is essential in inspiring others.

Embracing our blackness unites us

Picture yourself walking into a room with your natural curls, and you spot other black women rocking the same look. How quickly do you connect with them? That's the power of embracing your black beauty – it brings us together and creates a strong bond.

HISTORICAL AND CURRENT SOCIETAL CHALLENGES FACED BY BLACK WOMEN

The challenges faced by black women are real and deeply rooted in history. Many of these societal hurdles can be traced back to the days of slavery. Back then, we were seen as mere baby makers, objects for white men's pleasure, and extra hands for manual labor.

Add to that the legal restrictions that held women back in society, and the result was that black women had little to no opportunity to make meaningful contributions beyond these demeaning roles.

Though slavery has ended, we still carry the heavy burden of racism, poverty, and sexism in our patriarchal society.

This discrimination has had a significant impact on our earnings and opportunities in the workplace, creating a gender and racial wage gap between black women and others (including black men). It has also placed a glass ceiling on us, limiting our ability to reach our full potential in our careers.

When we bring these challenges down to the individual level, we find that many of us have internalized these misconceptions about black identity. These internalized beliefs have far-reaching consequences on our physical and mental health. As a result, too many black women are ashamed to embrace their identity, doubt their worth, or wait for others to validate them.

But, it's time for us to break free from these shackles and rise above the challenges. We are strong, capable, and deserving of every opportunity to thrive. Together, let's reclaim our power, embrace our identity, and show the world what black women are truly made of.

WAYS TO BUILD PRIDE AND CONFIDENCE IN YOUR BLACK IDENTITY

If we're sincere, the struggles we face as black women will not vanish overnight. We will have to adopt ways to fight them off by building pride and confidence in our identity.

Know the black race

Honey, take some time to do in-depth research about the black race. Listen to podcasts and shows, and read books authored by black people about the black race. You'll find that virtually all the reasons black folks are treated poorly compared to other humans are unfounded and false. Some of these reasons are mere assumptions that stemmed from the slavery of black people.

When you gain sufficient knowledge about your race and identity, you'll feel nothing but love and pride for your culture and the hurdles it had to overcome.

Racial socialization

It's hard, if not impossible, to love and have confidence in someone, something, or a system you know so little about. Well, the same can be said of the black race. Darling, you cannot establish confidence in your skin color when all you know about your race are the false stereotypes passed on to you.

Immersing yourself in your culture is a significant step in building pride and confidence in your black identity. Build interactions and meaningful relationships with other black folks, and attend functions, festivals, and concerts themed around the black culture. You'll never have reasons to hide or be ashamed of your identity again!

Get yourself a role model

Want to see reasons to develop pride in the black culture? Find a role model, a black woman representing the black race with dignity and doing exceptionally well in her field. You'd be proud to be associated with such a person, even by race.

Fall in love with a cultural element

If you have been made to detest the black race, I bet that was done with no valid evidence of something to be loathed about the black race, or because you heard something negative said about black people.

To prove that your race is worthy of your love, find something in the black culture to fall in love with. This can be food, music, fashion, or even language. And you can achieve this by exploring the different components of black culture until you find one thing that resonates with you.

Recognizing and Challenging Internalized Racism and Colorism

Sis, let me ask you a question. If you had the chance to be born again and choose your skin color, would you still choose to be black? If your answer is a heartfelt yes, then kudos to you – racism and colorism don't have a grip on your spirit. But if you're unsure or hesitant, it's okay, honey. It's a natural reaction to the negativity society has thrown at us over the years.

As we discussed in Chapter 4, internalized oppression – including racism – isn't a conscious choice. It's a product of our subconscious minds processing what we've been exposed to regularly. When you're constantly singled out because of your race, internalized racism can emerge from feelings of powerlessness.

But, sweetheart, it's our responsibility to recognize internalized racism and confront it head-on so we can live in the freedom we deserve as black women.

How do you spot internalized racism in your everyday life?

If you're afraid of embracing your ethnicity or try too hard not to conform to stereotypes about black people – like the "angry black woman" we talked about in Chapter 4 – then you might be harboring internalized racism.

When you avoid conversations about race or choose to stay neutral despite witnessing clear signs of racism, that avoidance could be a sign of internalized racism.

If you've ever used words like "archaic," "uncivilized," or "unsophisticated" to describe elements of black culture, you've likely been influenced by racial prejudice. And if you feel more comfortable around people from other races and distance yourself from fellow black people, it could be a sign of internalized racism.

Let's challenge these notions, embrace our blackness, and stand strong against the forces that try to bring us down. It's time to love ourselves fully and fiercely, unapologetically celebrating our black identity.

THE POWER AND BEAUTY OF BLACK CULTURE AND TRADITIONS

Let me tell you something – black is beyond beautiful! I'm not just repeating an old slogan from the 1968 movement. Our black identity is genuinely filled with awe-inspiring attributes that deserve admiration.

Our history tells a story of resilience. We rose from the dark times of slavery, when our skin and hair were deemed inferior, and fought for our freedom with the help of visionaries like Martin Luther King Jr. and Nelson Mandela. Even when society tried to suppress our creativity by forcing us to cover our hair, we didn't let that stop us, honey. We created stunning headgear, scarves, and hats that showcased our beauty and strength.

Now, we have black women like Oprah Winfrey, Michelle Obama, and Viola Davis breaking barriers and making history. The black race is a shining example of strength and resilience.

Our culture and traditions emphasize community, togetherness, and family. Life is so much richer when you're surrounded by love and support, and the black community excels at fostering a sense of belonging.

Let's not forget that our culture is built on respect and honor, values essential to preserving humanity. We're also deeply connected to nature, our ancestry, and spirituality, which guide us in leading morally upright lives and staying grounded.

So, my beautiful sister, let's revel in our blackness and embrace the magic we carry within us. It's time to stand tall and be proud of our rich heritage and remarkable journey.

Girl, aren't you just proud to be black?

TECHNIQUES FOR CULTIVATING A POSITIVE AND EMPOWERING SELF-IMAGE

Alright, we've reminded ourselves about the richness and beauty of the black race, but now it's time to focus on you. Embracing your black identity starts with cherishing yourself as a unique human being. Let's dive into some practical ways to build a healthy self-image and empower yourself to shine.

Care for your hair and skin with love: Choose routines and products that nurture your unique hair and skin type without compromising quality. Treat yourself like the queen you are!

Embrace your personality: Beyond your appearance, your personality traits make you extraordinary and beautiful. Discover what makes you uniquely you and appreciate those qualities.

Strive for excellence: Give your best in everything you do, and never settle for less. Being top-notch will help you see yourself through a lens of confidence and power.

Celebrate your wins unapologetically: Toot your own horn, honey! Celebrate your achievements and let the world know how amazing you are. This mindset will help you see yourself in a more positive light.

Break down imagined barriers: Understand that any perceived differences between you and someone of another race are mainly in our minds. While discrimination against melanin and 4c hair is real, there's no evidence to suggest that one race is superior to another. We all have unique strengths and qualities.

Separate your weaknesses from your race: Recognize that your flaws and shortcomings are not a result of your race. They're a part of being human. Embrace your imperfections and work on them as an individual, not as a reflection of your black identity.

By cultivating a positive self-image and empowering yourself, you'll be able to stand tall in your blackness and celebrate the incredible person you are.

THE IMPACT OF REPRESENTATION IN MEDIA AND POP CULTURE ON BLACK WOMEN

Sweetheart, it's no secret that the media and pop culture haven't always been kind to black women. Beauty standards have subtly leaned towards whiteness, suggesting that features closer to Western or European ideals like straight hair, thin nose, lips, and light skin tone are more beautiful. This skewed representation often leads to black girls growing up with trouble accepting themselves and their appearance.

But, honey, it's time for us to rise above these misrepresentations and embrace the unique qualities and talents we possess as black women. Here's how we can do that:

Affirm your greatness: Use daily affirmations to remind yourself of your unique talents and blessings. Your life will flourish when you embrace your uniqueness.

Speak up, girl: Don't let stereotypes or anyone hold you back from sharing your voice with the world. Your ideas and wisdom are essential, so speak up!

Step out of your comfort zone: To rise above racism and stereotypes, you've got to break free from what's comfortable. Try new things, explore new places, and go for that opportunity you never thought possible.

Embrace growth: Keep getting better, sis! The world can't ignore you when you're shining at the top. Always seek to improve and embrace change.

Don't wait for others: Don't sit around waiting for someone to recognize your unique talents and share them with the world. It's up to you to showcase your gifts, and social media gives you the platform to do so.

So, let's celebrate our uniqueness as black women and let our talents shine for all to see! With millions of people online, there's no better time to showcase the incredible, gifted black woman you are.

SUMMARY, ACTION STEPS & EXERCISES

- Reflect on your cultural identity and history. What aspects of your culture are most important to you? How can you incorporate those into your daily life?
- Seek out and connect with other black women in your community. Share your experiences and support each other.
- Practice self-care by setting boundaries and taking time for yourself. Remember, you deserve to rest and recharge.

I hope you're feeling more connected to your roots after reading this chapter. Celebrating and embracing our blackness is an essential aspect of our self-care journey, and it's something that should never be taken for granted. By taking the time to learn about our culture and find joy in our identity, we can better navigate the challenges of society and build confidence in ourselves.

We've discussed some of the techniques for building pride in our identity and navigating the unique challenges we face as black women. We've talked about the importance of exploring our cultural identity, building a community, and finding the courage to speak up against discrimination.

As you move forward in your journey, remember to continue building your connection to your identity, finding joy in your blackness, and taking care of yourself. Self-care isn't just about taking bubble baths and getting massages; it's about building a strong sense of self and finding pride in who you are.

Now, let's move on to the next chapter, where we'll talk about finding your purpose and passion in life. We all have unique talents and gifts that we can use to make a positive impact on the world, and it's time to explore what makes you feel alive and fulfilled. Let's dive in and find what ignites your soul, sis!

CHAPTER 12
FINDING YOUR PURPOSE AND PASSION

"The purpose of life is to live it, to taste experience to the utmost, to reach out eagerly and without fear for newer and richer experience." - Eleanor Roosevelt

H ey there beautiful, I'm so excited about your continued progress on this journey!

We'll start by defining what purpose and passion mean and why they matter. Next, we'll dive into techniques for discovering your purpose and passion, including reflection exercises and exploration of personal interests and values. Finally, we'll discuss how to build a life around your purpose and passion and make it a priority.

Our purpose and passion are what drive us forward, motivate us, and give us direction in life. This chapter will help you explore what those things mean to you and how to create a life around them.

It's a journey of self-discovery that will take time, but trust me, it's worth it.

You're about to have a clear roadmap for living a life that aligns with your values and brings you joy and fulfillment.

Time to grab your notebook again, because now we learn how to live our lives to the fullest and to reach our full potential.

DEFINING PURPOSE AND PASSION

Girl, the idea of finding your purpose has been around forever. It seems like every day there's a new life coach popping up, promising to help you discover your purpose. But here's the tea: we've been misled to think that we're not truly living our purpose unless we're doing something larger-than-life or gaining fame for our talents. And with everyone sharing their achievements on social media, it's easy to feel like you're the only one left in the dark.

But don't you worry. I'm here to help you understand what purpose really is, how to uncover yours, and step into it with confidence and grace.

What is Purpose?

Purpose has often been confused with hobbies, career success, and material possessions. But let me tell you, it's so much deeper than that. Your purpose is the reason you're here, the driving force behind your actions, and sometimes it takes looking beyond your accomplishments to truly see it.

Your purpose isn't just one big thing you do at a specific time. Instead, it's the underlying theme in all you do – your actions and the intentions behind them. It's the essence of your life's decisions, the relationships you nurture, and the impact you have on those around you.

Now, it's totally fine if fulfilling your purpose leads you to fame or recognition. But guess what? You can still live a purposeful life without being known beyond your immediate circle. It's okay to lead a quiet, peaceful life without millions of followers, as long as you're making life better for someone – even if that someone is you.

Passion is the emotional fuel that drives your purpose. It's the spark that lights your fire, the motivation that keeps you going, and the enthusiasm that propels your actions. Passions aren't your purpose, but they can be a powerful clue to discovering the difference you can make in the world.

Remember that purpose and passion are intertwined, and together, they'll guide you to a life full of meaning, fulfillment, and joy.

TECHNIQUES FOR DISCOVERING YOUR PURPOSE AND PASSION

As simple as the definition of purpose may sound, purpose discovery is anything but simple and straightforward. Truth be told, we are all different and unique, so there isn't a one-size-fits-all formula we can all use to discover our individual purpose and passions. However, there are practical techniques we can use to navigate this discovery and lead lives that are aligned with who we are.

Embark on your self-awareness journey

Let's break it down, sis. Imagine trying to figure out the purpose of a washing machine without having the slightest clue what it looks like or what it does. Sounds impossible, right? Well, the same goes for discovering our purpose – we can't genuinely grasp it without first developing a deep understanding of who we are and how we're wired.

So, to uncover your purpose, it's essential to dive deep into self-awareness and master your own unique essence. One powerful way to do this is by journaling. Write down your thoughts, actions, strategies, and energy – anything that helps you explore the depths of your being. By taking the time to study and reflect on your life's patterns, you'll be well on your way to understanding your purpose and making your mark on the world.

What's that inner voice yearning to express?

Your innate talents and abilities can guide you towards your purpose. You know, those things you do so effortlessly? Maybe it's connecting with new people, rocking at organizing, or offering others a shoulder to lean on. The list goes on.

But there's more. What are those activities you wish you had more time for? Or that one thing you're just dying to have a chance to do, especially if it enriches your life and those around you? If something comes to mind, girl, you might be staring your purpose right in the face.

Now, this isn't to say we won't pick up new skills along the way as we live purposefully. But that natural talent you possess (even if it requires some polishing) could be the key to unlocking the life you were meant to live.

Follow your passion

Passion and purpose go hand in hand. When you feel that fire in your belly, it's a sign that you're on the right track. What activities, causes, or topics make your heart sing? Take note of these passions and look for ways to incorporate them into your life. As you follow your passions, you'll likely find that they intersect with your purpose.

Tune in to what others observe about you

Now, this little technique is something I'm always excited to share with my sisters. We don't live our lives based on others' opinions, right? But sometimes, their insights can help us uncover our purpose. In Jim Scott's book "Radical Candor", he gives an in-depth look into this term "radical candor" where you ask for genuine, unbiased feedback from those you trust.

If you don't have a space for people to share their thoughts, create one! Reach out to a handful of close friends and ask them for an honest rundown of your life and what they've noticed truly matters to you.

Reflect and filter

While others' insights can help us see patterns and behaviors that point to our purpose, remember not to cling to every word they say or base your worth on their opinions. That's where filtering comes in.

The one person who can genuinely uncover your life's purpose is you. To do this, dive deep within yourself and unearth your true calling. Start by asking questions that can guide you on your journey of purpose discovery. What would an ideal world look like for me? What could I be happy doing for the rest of my life? What brings me joy and fulfillment, and does it benefit humanity and make life better for others?

Embrace each moment with intention

No more living on autopilot. When you live each moment deliberately, you take control and decide where to direct your energy. As a result, you can easily track where your energy is flowing. If that area improves others' lives, you're probably already living a purposeful life.

Find your tribe

Where do you feel truly at home? Who brings you peace and a sense of belonging? What's that one place where the world fades away and you're just present in the moment? (I'm not talking about your lover's arms, though.)

When you discover that space that keeps pulling at your heart-strings, make time to immerse yourself in it. Trust me, your purpose is closely intertwined with that place.

Put your vision into words

You'd be surprised how much of your purpose you already know, but it only becomes clear once you put it in writing.

Grab that journal of yours and write down your vision statement – the goals you want to achieve in your lifetime (that make a difference in the world). And if you're ready for some soul-searching, write your own eulogy. Your purpose will become clearer.

Embrace anger and frustration as guides

This last one might raise eyebrows, but it's true. Your anger and frustration can help you find your purpose.

You might be wondering, "How, Jada? Aren't those negative emotions? Does that mean my purpose is negative, too?" Absolutely not, honey. Let me explain.

Instead of dismissing your anger when you're upset at someone or a situation, analyze it. Dig into why you're feeling that way. If you find yourself constantly annoyed when younger black women conform to societal pressures, you might uncover a calling to help them embrace and celebrate their uniqueness.

That's my story right there. When I see my black sisters living beneath their potential, a wave of sadness overwhelms me. Sometimes I react in ways I'm not proud of. But upon examining that emotion, I realized it stemmed from my purpose: to uplift black women.

On the other hand, if you're feeling frustrated in your life, it might mean your future self is urging you to step into a higher version of your current self, which is likely in line with your purpose.

DISCOVERING MEANING AND FULFILLMENT

What does finding your purpose bring to your life?

Uncovering your purpose is like finding hidden treasure. It brings a deep sense of self-worth, knowing you have a significant role to play in this vast universe, and that your life matters enough to make a difference.

Embracing your purpose helps you break free from internalized racism and colorism – you realize your importance, even when the world doesn't recognize your beauty!

When your purpose aligns with your passion, you wake up each day with a fire in your soul. You won't need external motivation to maintain habits that keep you thriving because you can't imagine leaving this world without fulfilling your divine calling.

Finding your purpose ignites an unstoppable drive to achieve your goals. Each goal becomes a stepping stone on your purpose-driven path. You'll find yourself seizing every opportunity and nurturing every relationship, as your purpose sets a standard of excellence, you're eager to meet. The sense of meaning and fulfillment that comes with knowing your purpose is priceless.

Infusing Purpose and Values into Your Everyday Life

Discovering your purpose leads you to embrace the values that shape you and your outlook on life. But remember, uncovering your purpose and the values that support it is just the beginning of this beautiful journey.

The next step is to make your purpose and values an integral part of your daily life. By consciously anchoring your life on these values, you'll experience a more meaningful, fulfilling, and harmonious existence.

So, how do you weave your values into the fabric of your life? Keep them front and center, talk about them with passion, reaffirm them to yourself, and let them be the driving force behind your actions. When connecting with others, don't shy away from sharing your values and making them the foundation of your personal and professional boundaries.

By infusing your purpose and values into every aspect of your life, you'll create a powerful, authentic, and radiant version of yourself, ready to shine in this world!

SUMMARY, ACTION STEPS & EXERCISES

- Reflect on your personal values and interests.
- Write down what makes you feel most alive.
- Explore new hobbies or interests.
- Take steps to make your purpose and passion a priority in your life.

Look how far we've come! In this chapter, we went deep into the significance of discovering your purpose and passion in life.

Identifying the spark that ignites your soul is the first step towards crafting a life that's fulfilling and aligned with your values. We've shared some powerful techniques to help you uncover what sets your heart on fire and how to build a life centered around it.

We explored methods to uncover your purpose and passion, including journaling, embracing new experiences, and reflecting on the moments that bring you the most joy. We also touched on the importance of sculpting a life around your purpose and passion, highlighting how this path leads to a greater sense of satisfaction and success.

Remember, sis, finding your purpose and passion is a journey, and it's perfectly okay if it takes time to unravel the mystery of your calling. The key is to remain curious, continue exploring, and keep experimenting until you find what truly makes your soul sing.

CONCLUSION

"I am not afraid of storms, for I am learning how to sail my ship." - Louisa May Alcott

We have reached the end of this journey together. It has been an incredible experience to walk with you as we explored the importance of self-care and emotional empowerment for black women.

As we come to the end of this book, it's important to remember that our journey of self-love and growth is never over. It's an ongoing process that requires our continuous commitment and dedication.

You have discovered the techniques to challenge negative self-talk, make self-care a part of your daily routine, overcome internalized oppression, heal from past traumas, build and maintain healthy relationships, love your physical self, and achieve financial independence. You have learned the importance of building a support system, embracing and celebrating your blackness, finding your purpose and passion, and taking action to achieve your goals.

All these chapters have been leading you to one thing: prioritizing self-love. Self-love is the foundation of everything we've discussed. Without self-love, it's impossible to achieve anything else. You must cultivate self-love every day. It's a journey that never ends. You will always be evolving, growing, and learning new things about yourself.

Remember, we are in this together. And I want to encourage you to continue on this path of self-love and growth. Keep practicing self-care and mindfulness. Continue to challenge negative self-talk and overcome internalized oppression. Build healthy relationships and celebrate your blackness. Pursue your passions and dreams and set goals that align with your purpose. Celebrate your progress, and most importantly, continue to love and prioritize yourself.

I want to share with you a fun short story to wrap up this journey. It's about a girl who had been taking care of her mother, father, and younger sister since she was a teenager. She had always put her family first and herself last. She would help them with their needs and take care of the house while neglecting her own needs. She often felt drained and exhausted, but she kept going, thinking that she had to be strong for her family.

One day, she met a wise old woman who asked her how she was doing. The girl told her about her family and how she had been taking care of them for years. The old woman listened and then said to her, "My dear, you cannot pour from an empty cup. You must take care of yourself first so that you can take care of others."

The girl realized that she had been neglecting herself, and that taking care of herself was just as important as taking care of her family. She started setting boundaries and practicing self-care. She made time to do the things that made her feel happy and fulfilled.

She started to feel better, more energized, and more motivated to continue caring for her family.

Sis, I hope this short story resonates with you and reminds you that you cannot pour from an empty cup. You must prioritize self-care and emotional empowerment to be the best version of yourself.

I want to remind you that you are worthy, loved, and deserving of all the good things life has to offer. Never forget that. You have all the tools and knowledge you need to continue your journey of self-love and emotional empowerment. It's up to you to apply what you've learned in this book. I believe in you, and I am rooting for you every step of the way.

As Louisa May Alcott once said, "I am not afraid of storms, for I am learning how to sail my ship." You, too, can learn how to sail your ship and weather any storm that comes your way.

So, go out there and continue to conquer negative self-talk and internalized oppression, heal, grow, and thrive.

The journey of self-love never ends.

Keep sailing, sis!

Jada

REFERENCES

Winter M.F. (August 1, 2019). Demystifying Internalized Oppression: The Pain of Internalized Oppression. The Inclusion Solution. http://www.theinclusionsolution.me/demystifying-internalized-oppression-the-pain-of-internalized-oppression-biases-self-reflection/

Robbins T. The Secrets of Solving Disagreements In Relationships. Tony Robbins. https://www.tonyrobbins.com/ultimate-relationship-guide/resolve-conflict-save-relationship/

Dr. Cloud H. and Dr. Townsend J. (1992). Boundaries. Zondervan.

Earnshaw E. (December 13, 2022). 6 Types of Boundaries You Deserve to Have (and how to maintain them). MBG Relationships. https://www.mindbodygreen.com/articles/six-types-of-boundaries-and-what-healthy-boundaries-look-like-for-each

Asare J.G. (May 31, 2019). Overcoming the Angry Black Woman Stereotypes. Forbes. https://www.forbes.com/sites/janicegassam/2019/05/31/overcoming-the-angry-black-woman-stereotype/?sh=6f1a55a91fce

Community Tool Box. Cultural Competence: Healing from Internalized Oppression. Chapter 27. https://ctb.ku.edu/en/table-of-contents/culture/cultural-competence/healing-from-interalized-oppression/main

Jenkins S. (April 28, 2010). EMDR: A Symptom-Based Eight-Phased Treatment. Good Therapy. https://www.goodtherapy.org/blog/emdr-a-symptom-based-eight-phased-treatment/amp/

Mayoclinic Staff (December 13, 2022). Post Traumatic Stress Disorder. Mayoclinic. https://www.mayoclinic.org/diseases-conditions/post-traumatic-stress-disorder/symptoms-causes/syc-20355967

Moreno R. (August 11, 2022). What Is Body Positivity, and What Does It Mean In 2022?. Oprah Daily. https://www.oprahdaily.com/life/health/a40809665/what-is-body-positivity/

Eaton J. (June 3, 2020). What Black Women Should Know About Building Generational Wealth. Business Insider. https://www.businessinsider.com/personal-finance/what-want-black-women-know-about-building-generational-wealth-2020-6?r=US&IR=T

Herman A. And Murren H. (February 3, 2021). Invest In Black Women to Drive the Economy Forward. Fortune. https://fortune.com/2021/02/03/black-women-economy-diversity-equity-inclusion/amp/

Stanborough R.J. (November 25, 2020). What to Know About a Negative

REFERENCES

Body Image and How to Overcome It. Healthline. https://www.healthline.com/health/negative-body-image#signs-and-symptoms

Rosenfield J. (June 24, 2022). 8 Real Ways to Multiply Your Money. Yahoo Finance. https://finance.yahoo.com/news/8-real-ways-multiply-money-180045477.html

Taylor S.R. (2008). The Body Is Not An Apology: The Power of Radical Self-Love. Berrett-Koehler Publishers, Inc.

Dr. Lewis V. (2012). Positive Bodies: Loving the Skin You're In. Australian Academic Press.

Washington P. C. Real Money Answers for Every Woman: How to Win the Money Game With or Without a Man.

Hollis R. (2019). Girl, Stop Apologizing: Shame-Free Plan for Embracing and Achieving Your Goals. Harper Collins Leadership.

(September/October 1986). Black Women Face The 21st Century: Major Issues and Problems. The Black Scholar 17(5). Page 12.

Frye J. (August 22, 2029). Racism and Sexism Combine to Shortchange Black Women. The American Progress. https://www.americanprogress.org/article/racism-sexism-combine-shortchange-working-black-women/

Kher S. (November 28, 2018) 10 Practical Tips for Women In the Corporate World. LinkedIn. https://www.linkedin.com/pulse/10-practical-tips-women-corporate-world-suman-kher

Amara H. (2017). Awaken Your Inner Fire. Heirophant Publishing.

McKay M., Forsyth J.P., and Eifert G. H. (2010). Your Life On Purpose: How to Find What Matters, Create the Life You Want. New Harbinger Publications, Inc.

Villarosa L. (August 14, 2019). Myths About Physical Racial Differences. The New York Times. https://www.nytimes.com/interactive/2019/08/14/magazine/racial-differences-doctors.html

Johnson V.E. and Carter R.T. (December 3, 2019). Black Cultural Strength and Psychological Well-Being: An Empirical Analysis with Black American Adults. The Association of Black Psychologists 46(1).

Jim Scott. (2017). Radical Candour: How to Get What You Want By Saying What You Mean. St. Martin's Press.

Bryant S.L. The Beauty Ideal: The Effects of European Standards of Beauty on Black Women. Columbia Social Work Review IV.

www.ingramcontent.com/pod-product-compliance
Lightning Source LLC
Chambersburg PA
CBHW020254130626
46549CB00005B/2216